making waves

**TWR's journey to reach the world
for Christ through media**

Richard Greene and John Lundy

Making Waves

*TWR's Journey to Reach the World
for Christ Through Media*

by Richard Greene and John Lundy

ALL RIGHTS RESERVED
Copyright © 2024 Trans World Radio

ISBN: 9798877321922

twr.org

P.O. Box 8700
Cary, NC 27512

PUBLISHED IN THE UNITED STATES OF AMERICA

Contents

SECTION V
THE WAVE OF THE FUTURE   185

4

Foreword

Dr. Erwin W. Lutzer

YOU HOLD IN your hands a story of vision, innovation and proof of the power of the gospel.

Since its inauspicious first broadcast in February 1954, the ministry of Trans World Radio (TWR) has consistently proven that with prayer, technical expertise and a burden for people who are spiritually lost, a small vision can become an ever-expanding worldwide vision.

When God created the universe, he included in it a phenomenon that centuries later would enable technicians to create radio waves; these are defined as a type of electromagnetic radiation capable of carrying signals such as human voices virtually all over the world.

I personally rejoice that I don't have to understand how these work to benefit from them. I can just flip the dial on a radio or click on a podcast to listen to someone (frequently someone I have never met) share their wisdom.

Trans World Radio makes waves.

Several years ago, my wife, Rebecca, and I participated in a tour of Europe along with some of the leadership of TWR. What we learned has stayed with me; in fact, in many ways, having read this book, I see more clearly than ever the unique outreach God has given to this effective global ministry.

Come with me and visit an undisclosed location in Europe whose rooms are filled with computers, maps and other digital equipment installed by a gifted team that understands what it takes to get the radio signals across borders into "closed" countries. Then, visit ministry offices where teams of people answer queries in various languages, praying with the needy and sending literature to disciple men and women and children. Despite diverse responsibilities, each team member of TWR shares the same heartbeat, the same vision and desire that the gospel would reach even more people around the world.

Giving oversight to all the present ministries and future expansion are President Lauren Libby and his team, who troubleshoot when problems arise; they strategize, asking themselves what they can do next to expand the ministry. Do they have funds to increase the wattage of a station somewhere in a remote corner of the world? Or what will it take to build a new station when an older one has been damaged by war or a natural disaster? Or how do they reach still more using today's technological advances? The challenges are endless and made even more so because they abide by their policy of not going into debt. And that is why TWR moves forward on its knees.

Moody Church Media has partnered with TWR for many years, and we can say with certainty that this is a ministry that has integrity and vision, and above all, we rejoice that TWR reaches millions of people with the gospel – more than we ever hear about. For every testimony in this book, there are thousands of other people we don't hear from but who have come to faith in Christ and have grown in their walk with God through TWR's ministry. God never allows us to see all the good we do. Heaven awaits a full accounting.

Paul Freed could never have imagined that what he began in 1954 would become the international ministry that TWR is today. And with advances in technology, including video and online, the present leadership at TWR may not be able to imagine what lies ahead for this growing ministry. Lauren Libby reminds us that "With God all things are possible to those who believe."

God grant that it shall be so.

Dr. Erwin W. Lutzer, Pastor Emeritus • The Moody Church, Chicago

Acknowledgments

THE JOYFUL WORK of writing *Making Waves* has been made possible by dozens of people who contributed in multiple ways.

The authors would like to thank TWR leadership, starting with President and CEO Lauren Libby, who had the vision for this book and graciously entrusted us to write it. We also gratefully acknowledge Tim Klingbeil and David McCreary for their steady guidance and constant support.

We got rolling from the outset when Julia Hall provided a bevy of reports on multiple projects covered extensively in this book. These provided a wealth of updates and background material.

Early on, Rachel Mehlhaff took a detailed look at the book and provided invaluable midcourse corrections, particularly from the perspective of younger readers. Thanks to Dennis Walker, who spent many hours researching data about the Roma people and many more hours exploring TWR archives for the best possible photos to illustrate this book. And we want to express our gratitude for the vital contributions of our principal editor, Jon Hill, who improves everything he touches with care, sensitivity, precision and top-of-the-line professionalism.

We're also grateful to the TWR design team of Jeannine Klingbeil and Nicole Hughes. They used great skill and diligence in designing a striking cover and giving this book a cohesive and attractive appearance. Special thanks to Ellen Salas for formatting and producing our first physical edition.

Our heartfelt thanks also go to the following individuals who sat for interviews – in person or online or by phone – or provided much-needed information, consultation and/or assistance without which the writing of this book would have been impossible: Aicha,* Darin Alvord, Nathan Anderson, James Baker, Mike Ball, Peggy Banks, Joe Barker, Lonnie Berger, Branko Bjelajac, Park Sang Bum, Bill Damick, Morgane Erisman, Jon Fugler, Bernice Gatere, Tyler Gates, Paul Harkness, Ledi Hibibasi, Scott A. Jones, Garth Kennedy, Aaron Tan, Werner Kroemer, Samuel Lacho, Esteban Larrosa, Jonathan Lee, Eugene Lim, Candace Mackie, Bill Mial, Alberto González Muñoz, Sphiwe Nxumalo-Ngwenya, Juliet Oppong-Amoako, Sterling Ottun, John Owens, Dave Pedersen, Caleb Petersen,* Marietjie Prollius, Brother Rachid, Daryl Renshaw, Abdoulaye Sangho, Daniel Saputra,* Hirotaka Sasaki, Luiz Sayão, Nick Siemens, Larry and Patti Souder, Steve Stavropoulos, Ralf Stores, Tom Streeter, Junki Sugiyama, John Summerville, Leanne Tan, Samuel Tan, Malise Terrell, Annabel Torrealba, Tom Watkins, Maria Wedel, Carlos Yepes and Kimberly Yepes.

We could not have completed this book without the studio expertise of Andy Napier. He not only agreed to be interviewed himself, but also gave us access to previous interviews he had done with TWR leaders, and he recorded Lauren Libby on three occasions to glean from him critical – and inspirational – stories of God's wondrous handiwork and provision around the world. And thanks to Craig Slater for his assistance in lining up those presidential interviews.

Above all, we give thanks and praise to the Holy Spirit, who gives wisdom and counsel; our Lord and Savior Jesus Christ, who redeemed us; and God the Father, who has been making waves since before the world began.

Pseudonyms are used for security reasons.

"One generation will praise your works to another,

and will declare your mighty acts."

— PSALM 145:4

Introduction

TRANS WORLD RADIO (TWR) has been proclaiming the wondrous good news of Jesus Christ since February 1954. From the very beginning, we have declared with conviction and clarity that the One True God created the universe and then us in his likeness to have fellowship with him. But Adam and Eve disobeyed God's commands, and their relationship with him was broken. Sin and death entered the world and, as a result, all humankind are born with a sin nature. Therefore, we, too, are bent toward sin and are separated from God. And because God is holy and pure, we deserve his punishment. But God's good news is that he still loves us and that he sent his one and only Son on a rescue mission to die for our sins. Though perfect, having never sinned himself, Jesus took the penalty and payment for our sins when he was nailed to a cross. And, as was promised, on the third day – that first Easter – God raised Christ from the dead, and he is alive today. We can know him through the Scriptures and follow him as Lord through the power of the Holy Spirit, but only if we put our trust in him by faith.

TWR came into existence for this very reason, and our missionaries and staff remain committed to spreading this glorious gospel around the world until Jesus returns as King of Kings and Lord of Lords. Whether through original programming or teaming with other Christian leaders and ministries to translate their broadcasts into local, indigenous languages, TWR treasures each opportunity to herald God's love and grace to the whole world.

Two memoirs capture TWR's ministry. *Towers to Eternity*, written by founder Paul E. Freed, chronicles the early years of how God raised up and expanded and extended this international outreach. *Great Things He Has Done*, filled with inspirational anecdotes from longtime missionary Bill Mial, is a testimony of God's faithfulness throughout our history.

So why this book? Why now?

Though we especially highlight the many upgrades, expansions and new ministry initiatives that have occurred in the past 15 years or so, this is not a history book. And though we celebrate a host of anniversaries throughout these pages, this is not an anniversary book. And it's not a third memoir.

So what is it?

We view it more as an instrumental faith story. God gave a vision to Dr. Freed, who set out to execute it. Instead of following in his father's footsteps as a missionary in the Middle East, he instead sensed something new and riveted his attention on the people of Spain who needed Jesus. Then the Lord broadened that vision to other regions of the world. Lives were being changed across the globe.

But the story didn't stop there. Still energized by God's Holy Spirit, it continues today. We're still learning that when God calls an organization, he goes to work!

Step by step – year after year – our team has had to look to God and to trust him to fulfill his mighty promises from the Bible. He has orchestrated events and guided us to the right people in the right places at the right times, providing the resources and the people to fulfill his will. Our team members worldwide continue to depend upon the Lord to forge ahead to bring hope among the world's nations, tribes, peoples and tongues – no matter what that decision to follow Jesus may cost them!

We have grown to become what our president, Lauren Libby, describes as "a big voice for Jesus."

"When you look at what the Lord has done over the past 15 years, basically we have doubled our broadcast coverage," he notes. "And he's wondrously and faithfully provided millions of dollars to do that through a global family of large and small donors alike. We acknowledge his unique handiwork."

God has called us to proclaim the good news of Jesus Christ to the whole world by mass media so that lasting fruit is produced. The gifting and calling are irrevocable. Within our calling, the Lord wants us to be spiritual entrepreneurs. We're to pray and step out in search of opportunities to serve, and, as we do, God will open doors to proclaim the mystery of Christ (Colossians 4:3) and help us to fulfill his will.

We keep partnering with his believers around the world to help fulfill his Great Commission to make disciples of all nations. This means we're willing to echo the words of the apostle Paul, that we, too, aspire "to preach the gospel, not where Christ was already known by name, so that I would not build on another person's foundation; but just as it is written: 'They who have not been told about Him will see, and they who have not heard will understand'" (Romans 15:20-21).

God has graciously blessed this ministry. We're on the air, online and on the ground, and we don't want to be found guilty of merely managing this growth. No, we're asking God to use us to do even more! We're still on mission.

Overall, we hope this book will encourage you to pursue God in an even deeper way. That these events and testimonies will fire up your own thinking as to how God wants to use you to reach men, women, boys and girls with the message of God's unfailing love. We pray that the Lord will use our journey to help you discover your unique role in advancing God's kingdom. Of some 8 billion people now in the world, at least 3 billion reportedly still need to hear for the first time the message of eternal salvation through Christ alone.

Jesus has not revoked his compassion for the multitudes. No one is outside his grace. His harvest remains plentiful, but the workers are still few. You can make a lasting difference for his cause.

So, as you read these pages, take some time to prayerfully consider these questions:

- How do you sense the Holy Spirit moving within you?

- What are you passionate about, and what do you need to fulfill the vision to which God is calling you?

- What are you trusting him for to help further his kingdom?

- Do you have family or friends who need to hear about Jesus – from you? Is it possible that the Lord is leading you to serve him in a distant land among people who still haven't had the gospel presented to them?

May TWR's story embolden you and even equip you to follow Jesus more closely and lead the ministry to which he has called you – whatever that may be and wherever he may take you.

We can't live the Christian life and obey God's voice on our own. Jesus has made that clear: "I am the vine, you are the branches; the one who remains in Me, and I in him bears much fruit, for apart from Me you can do nothing" (John 15:5).

But thank God that Philippians 4:13 is also true! "I can do all things through him who strengthens me."

From Day 1, the Lord has enabled TWR to launch out, even though on many occasions we couldn't see what awaited us around the corner. We had to trust him. And God proved himself faithful.

He will do the same for you!

So we hope this book will inspire you to take similar steps of faith, looking to the Lord for wisdom, grace, direction and power. He will always be with you, through thick and thin. He will answer prayer and provide for you – just as he has done for us. You can count on him!

Let God write your story to his glory!

SECTION I

The First Wave

PAUL FREED DIDN'T start out as a radio proponent. He believed God wanted him to serve as a missionary. But radio became the wave of the future when he realized the vast potential for reaching people for Jesus Christ. A new ministry took root in 1954 and started making waves – in Spain, then beyond.

"He has not dealt with us according to our sins,

nor rewarded us according to our iniquities.

For as high as the heavens are above the earth,

so great is His lovingkindness toward those who fear Him.

As far as the east is from the west,

so far has He removed our transgressions from us."

— PSALM 103:10-12

1

Rescued From a Notorious Drug Kingpin

CARLOS YEPES' WALLET was empty. Not a single peso. His kitchen staff had just pressed him about restocking their food shelves, but he urged them not to worry. God would provide once again, as he always had. The children they were ministering to – high-risk kids displaced by violence – would not go hungry.

The Lord had led Carlos to launch this children's outreach among impoverished families in a depressed neighborhood in downtown Bogotá, Colombia. These families, some of whom were headed by single moms, lived in houses cobbled together from boxes and pieces of scrap plastic. Hunger and misery were their constant companions.

When he met them, Carlos first rallied the kids around soccer. Next came feeding them and finally opening a school for them. His dream was to keep them off the streets and away from the clutches of slimy drug lords, whose tentacles often reached into such neighborhoods. He was all too familiar with that lifestyle, having been sucked in himself before being miraculously rescued and saved.

"Everybody wanted to take their kids to our ministry because of their hunger," Carlos said. "It was a river of people."

Trusting in God was becoming a way of life for Carlos. That's how this outreach began. Even though he didn't have the funds to secure a building to get everything off the ground, Carlos looked to God in faith to fulfill the promises he made in the Bible to make provision. He prayed, and God impressed upon a man – unknown to Carlos – to call him and say he had heard about the children and wanted to lend a hand. The man, who remained anonymous, wrote a check to cover the expenses to buy the building.

"We began with 120 kids, and we stepped out in obedience to God's calling," Carlos said.

The ministry kept growing. Now Carlos was looking to God for another miracle, providing food for 180 children.

After his staff left his office, he closed the door and cried out to God. "Lord, there is nothing, there is no money. Come to our aid!"

The doorbell rang. The kids were not accustomed to having doorbells at their houses, so they all jumped out of their classroom chairs and ran to the front door. They ushered in a well-dressed tall man and pointed him toward Carlos' office.

When he heard a knock at his door, Carlos pushed away from his desk and opened the door. There stood the man.

"Are you the pastor here?" the man asked.

"Yes," Carlos said.

"Pastor, I know you are going through some worries about the children's food."

How did he know this? Carlos wondered.

"I have a truck outside filled with food. Can you help unload it?"

Carlos rushed outside. It was crammed with bags of rice and beans, containers of oil, cartons of eggs – and so much more.

He and the children carried the food to the pantry. When the job was almost done, Carlos went to thank the man. With the keys to the truck dangling in his hand, the man said, "Pastor, don't ever be worried. God does not leave you. He is always taking care of you."

Carlos went back inside to assist the children with the final boxes. *Oh, I have to warn the man to be careful about some terrible potholes in the street,* Carlos thought.

But the man was gone, as was his truck. "He simply disappeared," Carlos said. He smiled, shook his head in amazement and looked heavenward. "Bless you, Jesus!"

CARLOS, TOO, HAD grown up poor in Colombia, one of 15 boys. He certainly knew about hunger.

But as a teenager and then as a young man in his early 20s, looking to God to fill his stomach – or to meet any other need for that matter – was furthest from his mind. Instead, he relied upon his own ingenuity and craftiness to stay alive as he'd become a trusted confidant and purveyor of illicit drugs alongside the notorious kingpin Pablo Escobar of the Medellín cartel.

Carlos became filthy rich!

That journey started when he was only 13 years old. "I left home looking for new horizons," Carlos told TWR staff members who visited him in 2019 to capture his story on video.

He made his way to Colombia's fertile coffee district. But he quickly grew tired of that crop and relocated to Bogotá, where he wanted to study and make something of his life. While earning his high school degree, he worked at a restaurant, frequented he said by ruffians.

"I was 15 and was running the restaurant because I showed to have responsibility," Carlos explained. "Everybody used to get really drunk, and I was the only sober one."

Carlos moved to Santa Marta on the west coast and ran into clients from the restaurant. They offered to pay his hotel bill if he would come to work for them. He took their bait. Before long, at the age of 17, he was planting and cultivating marijuana. He excelled at it.

Two years later, Carlos was harvesting coca leaves. Then he graduated to producing cocaine. His excellent product drew attention, especially from Escobar and his crime partner Carlos Lehder. The young Carlos Yepes' skills were so valued, up to 50 men were assigned to protect him – then only 21 years old!

At one point, Carlos made a trip to an isolated plantation in the mountains of northern Colombia. An avid reader, he usually brought a pile of books with him. But on this trip, his protection detail failed to pack them. He was furious and threatened to leave. But a woman on the plantation gave him the only book she had – a New Testament that also contained the Book of Proverbs. Carlos read it every night of the 20 days he was there. When it was time to leave, the woman insisted that he keep it.

Proverbs fascinated Carlos. He was so impressed with its practical wisdom that he started reading it to his bodyguards – every night! They, too, were intrigued.

"We made cocaine, we were armed, but during the night we read the New Testament," Carlos said, laughing. "We became something weird."

One harvesting season Carlos was exploring a mountainous site for a new plantation. He had let his bodyguards off to visit their families, so he was by himself, something he had not enjoyed for so long. "I felt free and awesome," he said. "It was a miracle for me to be alone."

But that decision almost cost him his life. While hacking away brush with a machete, he cut his leg. The deep gash bled profusely, filling his boot. He couldn't walk. He couldn't call for help. He started dragging himself back to the compound. Four hours later, he reached a couch.

Daylight disappeared and night descended, yet nobody came. Though now bandaged, his leg was swollen, and he was writhing in pain. Carlos pulled out the only solace he could find in the cabin: a small radio. As he fiddled with the dial, he came to the news. Afterward came a song about the Bible, catching him off guard. But it soothed his anxious spirit. "It brought to mind those many times we read the New Testament," he recalled.

Then a voice of hope met him on this desolate mountain.

"Several times I thought the preacher was right next to me, telling me everything," Carlos reflected.

God's love tugged at his heart.

"You won't find security in anything or anyone else but Christ," the preacher said. "There's no safety without Christ. Stop running. Say this prayer with me."

At that very moment, Carlos surrendered his life to Jesus. He prayed to accept him as Savior.

"To receive Jesus was incredible," he said, wiping both eyes. "A weight was lifted off my shoulders. I felt peace like never before. Christ came to the jungle and rescued me! I really found Jesus – or he found me. I think it is the second one."

In the cabin, Carlos rose gingerly to his feet and shuffled to a shower. He washed his leg and rebound his wound. He was so happy he couldn't sleep all night.

But Carlos knew he faced a monumental decision. He looked out over the cocaine plantation and started talking to God. "I want to follow you. What do we do?"

At around noon the next day, his bodyguards returned. They saw Carlos's condition and were afraid because they had been away when he needed them. "Please forgive us," they pleaded.

Carlos assured them that he was OK – and that they were OK, too.

But he told them that he had decided the night before to follow Jesus and that his life had changed. Then he really shocked them.

"I don't need cocaine anymore," he said. "I promised God that if I started walking soon, I would leave the cocaine world."

They were stunned.

Three days later, still resolute, Carlos poured gasoline over his whole cocaine operation and set it on fire. Staring into the blaze, he rejoiced. "That was that. Free from cocaine, free from the cocaine lab, free from everything!"

Rumors quickly circulated that Carlos had gone completely mad. His band of bodyguards wanted to know the location of that radio station to which he had listened. *That was the culprit*, they thought, *the thing that changed his thinking so drastically.*

But what they didn't know was that the program emanated from the Caribbean island of Bonaire, more than hundreds of miles away

But as they saw that Carlos' radical change was sticking, they wanted to know why.

So together they chose to listen with Carlos to another broadcast. Had they, too, gone crazy?

When the preacher got to the end, he challenged his listeners to pray to give their hearts to Christ. The men sat silent.

"They were scared for their future," Carlos remembered. "What would they do next? They were trained to be mercenaries. So now what?"

Carlos hammered home the need to commit their lives to Jesus and that the Lord would take care of them. He stood amazed, in awe of God, as man after man gave his heart to Christ.

They sold their guns. They planted coffee. They gave away everything. Ministry became their newest and utmost priority.

Carlos became a pastor and began serving his fellow Colombians. He'd tell them about Jesus and then help converts mature in their relationship with Christ. Small groups sprang up, with some leaders going on to biblical institutes.

But the growth didn't stop there. To date, Carlos has planted 25 churches. And he's continuing to use soccer to reach the youth of Bogotá – as well as feeding and educating them. His son has helped 20 churches form worship teams. His daughter Kimberly creates content for social media with TWR's national partner in Colombia and is one of the voices for the Spanish production of *Mission 66*, a contemporary Bible-survey course that originated in Brazil and that TWR is preparing to release in the world's 10 most-spoken languages.

And his former bodyguards? Well, 14 are now pastors. "They've spread out everywhere," Carlos said.

All because of the gift of a New Testament and a transistor radio tuned to Trans World Radio's powerful AM station on a small Caribbean island!

NOT ONLY IS the gospel transforming people throughout the Spanish-speaking world, but its message is also ringing true across the globe.

Today, now known as TWR, the farthest-reaching Christian media organization in the world is speaking hope and bearing lasting spiritual fruit among men, women, boys and girls – just like Carlos and his former bodyguards – in more than 190 countries and over 200 languages.

And it's not just radio. TWR is taking advantage of other technologies, including online streaming platforms, social media and video.

That's what this remarkable story is really about: using every means available, under the power and leading of God's Holy Spirit, to spread the light and good news of Jesus, that all might come to know him and bring him glory throughout all eternity.

TWR's staff remain committed to trusting God to use them to teach the Bible faithfully and to minister to audiences no matter what these listeners are experiencing in life – from persecution to pandemics.

Have there been bumps and discouragement along the way? Without question. It hasn't been all peaches and cream. There have been lots of pits in those peaches along the way, as TWR President Lauren Libby likes to say.

And yet, God's hand has been evident. He has intervened with encouraging victory after victory – and amazing miracles – as well. God's promises are forever true, and the Lord has remained faithful. He keeps providing the resources and raising up highly skilled and motivated people, fervent about fulfilling Christ's Great Commission to take the gospel to the ends of the earth. And lives continue to change.

So how did it all start?

"Let the people praise You, O God;

let all the peoples praise You.

Let the nations be glad and sing for joy;

for You will judge the peoples with uprightness

and guide the nations on the earth."

— PSALM 67:3-4

2

Lasting Fruit, Beginning in Spain

A N OLDER GENTLEMAN opened his front door and warmly greeted Dr. Paul Freed into his home in Seville, Spain – a major city located in the southwest corner of the country and known for its flamboyant flamenco dancing and architectural designs.

"Thank you for coming," the man said. "I am so honored."

He ushered Dr. Freed and his interpreter into his living room. Before speaking, Dr. Freed glanced around the room. He spotted a large radio and inquired about it. The man jumped up and couldn't wait for Dr. Freed to listen to what had become his favorite station.

He turned the radio on, and it came alive with songs of joy, followed by powerful teaching from the Bible. Words of hope and peace.

"I enjoy these programs deeply," the man told Dr. Freed. "They're dear to my heart. I did not know Christ before. Now I do. Heaven will be my home. Thank God for The Voice of Tangier."

Tears welled in Dr. Freed's eyes.

He had launched this new ministry in February 1952, founded under the name "International Evangelism." The associated Voice of Tangier broadcasts began in the same month two years later. They emanated from Tangier, Morocco, 153 miles away. So here Dr. Freed was visiting with a faithful listener in the man's home, hearing how the broadcasts were making an eternal difference not only in his life but also in the lives of others.

The older man didn't want to keep the good news just to himself. He began inviting some of his friends to listen to the broadcasts with him, and a small group started meeting regularly.

And he urged his wife to listen with him as well. Her heart grew warm to God's love.

The next day, Dr. Freed spoke at a small church on the edge of town. In the audience was the man's wife. That afternoon, after Dr. Freed's message about God's unending grace, she accepted Jesus Christ as her Savior. She and her husband cried together. And heaven rejoiced!

Paul Freed embraced radio as the most effective way to reach Spain, with its mountainous terrain and hundreds upon hundreds of remote communities.

God opened a door to Spain through radio broadcasting from North Africa, and soon Paul Freed saw responses from listeners pouring in.

"Early the next morning, we had to leave Seville," Dr. Freed said. "But how I wish I could have stood by the river, where she was baptized."

With deep thanks to God, Dr. Freed noted in a newsletter to financial and prayer supporters about these new believers: "I said in my heart that all the work, headaches and sacrifices were worth it a thousand times over."

What's phenomenal is that this ministry to Spain in the mid-1950s almost never took place.

PAUL FREED AND his sister, Ruth, grew up in the Middle East, the children of missionary parents, Ralph and Mildred Freed. They witnessed firsthand how their father and mother patiently and lovingly – yet forthrightly and boldly – presented the gospel to their friends in Palestine and Syria. Conversions can be rare in that region of the world, but together as a family, they praised God for how he worked in people's hearts and drew some to himself as they heard and responded to God's Word.

As young Paul grew in his own relationship with Christ, he prayerfully sensed the Lord leading him to surrender to God's calling to serve in missions.

But where and with whom? And how? Some unexpected answers came in Switzerland.

Paul had been educated in Jerusalem and Beirut before returning to the United States, where he attended Wheaton College in Illinois and Nyack Missionary Training Institute in New York. In 1948, he assumed the directorship of Youth for Christ in Greensboro, North Carolina.

That same year, Youth for Christ held its first of 12 congresses on world evangelization in August in Beatenberg, Switzerland. Organizers believed these meetings would be the catalyst used of God to bring about the complete and final evangelization of the world in their generation.

Hundreds of delegates from across the globe – many fresh from the battlefields of World War II – were invited to attend. Torrey Johnson, president of Youth for Christ International, exhorted the 30-year-old Dr. Freed, "I believe God would have you go to Europe." So he went.

Drawing on materials from the congress, a seminary professor of church history wrote that the participants were reminded they were not there "for a vacation ... or to trifle with time and opportunity. The Holy Spirit brought us together for Prayer, for Bible Study, for heart-searching and for waiting upon God. May it please HIM to give us a new and greater insight into the task of world evangelization and the means by which it can be accomplished NOW!"

Speaker after speaker challenged the attendees to "go from the Alpine heights of Beatenberg down to the world of men. ... May it please GOD through this conference to do a 'new thing' in our day."

While searching for God's leading, Dr. Freed met two "zealous" delegates from Spain. They vocalized the monumental and pressing need to reach their 30 million countrymen with the gospel of Jesus Christ. Despite the odds, they were sold out to the task. They were pleading for someone to come help them. How could they hear unless someone tells them?

Spain? Dr. Freed mused. It wasn't exactly on his missionary radar. So much so, he often said, "I was NOT interested in Spain," adding: "Spain was the most unlikely country for me – after an exciting childhood spent in Arab lands."

But as these two delegates persisted, he reluctantly agreed to go – with a "very puny" yes. He would look and explore the prospects.

With the Beatenberg congress fresh in his rearview mirror, Dr. Freed took a train to Barcelona. As he disembarked at the station, he noticed a red and yellow flag of Spain flapping in the breeze. *"God, why have you led me in this direction?"* he questioned.

God would clearly show him!

First off, the more Dr. Freed saw of Spain, the more he was taken by its potpourri of breathtaking landscapes. Its glistening, sandy subtropical coastlines, picturesque fielded plateaus and lofty, imposing snowcapped mountains captivated him.

But as alluring as Spain's natural beauty was, something much more endearing and deeper truly was capturing his heart. What thrilled him most was spending time with Spain's wonderful people and hearing their life stories, their dreams and aspirations, but also their challenges.

One of the first people God would choose to join Paul Freed's team in Tangier was Bill Mial, shown above. This began a career with TWR that would span more than six decades.

"A newcomer among the Spaniards, I found myself responding to their courtesy, their friendly inquisitiveness, their dignity, and their respect for human values," Dr. Freed wrote in his memoir *Towers to Eternity*. "Perhaps it was the impact of all these qualities reaching out to me that created my profound response to the Spanish people."

A kaleidoscope of humanity fascinated him. "Along the city streets, crowded with old women in black, selling chickens and figs and chestnuts and peppers, I heard the rattle of mule carts and wagons," he said. "I smelled the scent of orange blossoms and hot frying shrimp.

"Through intricate iron lace gates, I could see cattle barons, olive magnates, orange and cork kings sipping sherry, resting in cushioned chairs, far removed from the crowds in the street," he added.

But outside on the cobblestones, the "other half" tugged at Dr. Freed. Farmers. Shopkeepers. Peasants. Dockhands. Beggars. Gypsies. Vendors. Children, many clamoring for handouts. "Slight, agile people, knowing and cynical, yet so appealing to me with their dark eyes and sudden smiles."

An "inexplainable concern" was growing in his heart.

Dr. Freed, however, was much more than an avid people-watcher and engaging conversationalist. That *concern* extended far beyond his stimulating encounters with various societal strata. It's what kept him up at night – and on his knees. And it's what energized him.

"To be very candid, it seemed that what motivated me so strongly to help the Spanish Christians was the sturdiness of the believer I met wherever I visited – from the Pyrenees villages in the north to sunny Andalusia on the Mediterranean," he reflected.

"It seemed that God was asking me to help them multiply their spiritual blessings in order to reach others of their own people with a positive gospel message," he further said. "I gradually realized that these people, in whom I had never had any personal interest, were burdened with needs equally as great as the Arab people I had grown up with and whom I had longed to serve."

Throughout that first exploratory trip, whether in cities or hamlets, Dr. Freed took part in evangelistic services. He had the privilege on multiple occasions to proclaim the message of salvation through Christ alone.

"The interest was keen wherever I went, and the whole time I was there, I never once spoke to an empty seat," he said. "In fact, often the chairs were removed to make room for more of the hungry of heart. No matter where I went, the needs were urgent."

Dr. Freed once penned: "As we drove over mile after mile of dusty, hot side roads, you will never know the thrill of swinging down a mountainside and seeing village after village where there were dear people who never before had heard the gospel."

But how could still more of them hear of the goodness of God? His father had been his model for evangelism. Ralph Freed was certainly gifted in personal, one-on-one conversations. The big question confronting – if not haunting –Paul Freed was how could millions who were unfamiliar with the claims of Christ be reached?

As he said goodbye to his new Spanish friends, he told them that he would pray about what his personal responsibility would be to coming alongside them and co-laboring with them to proclaim God's good news.

Once back home in Greensboro, Dr. Freed pondered the possibilities. Two of the biggest and most complex challenges would be Spain's mountainous terrain and hundreds upon hundreds of remote communities.

The more he prayed, the more the answer became clear. "There was only one answer in my mind to the problem. Radio," he said. "Like nothing else, radio could blanket the nation from peak to valley, from inland Madrid to coastal Cadiz."

Though he did not have "a dime of support" or know "what steps to take," Dr. Freed was convinced that the Lord had unambiguously "linked my heart to the heart of Spain" and that he wanted him to step out by faith in obedience and be part of the evangelistic solution.

But the religious and political climate of the day would present new obstacles as to how Dr. Freed and Spanish believers could possibly establish a broadcasting presence within Spain's borders. During the strict regime of General Francisco Franco, church and state issues set up multiple barriers that would prevent them from operating radio stations and broadcasting within the country. Only the Catholic Church had that right.

Discouraged, but not daunted, the group prayed, and God opened an unlikely door in North Africa, two dozen miles across the Strait of Gibraltar in Tangier, Morocco. At first, though, Dr. Freed balked at this suggestion, confounded by the idea of broadcasting *to* Spain from *outside* of Spain instead of *within* Spain.

But he and his six-person team took a ferry to Morocco, then trekked up into the mountains for a picnic at sunset. There, as they stood on Moroccan soil and gazed across the water, they saw Spain. At that moment, they realized there was "freedom here to build, whereas there might never be an opportunity in Spain."

In a fragrant pine grove, the group "knelt and asked God to give us the desire of our hearts – that we might be used to bridge the straits with a clear signal of the good news of Jesus Christ for the Spanish people."

God had knit their hearts together with a "passion to tell all those people that Jesus Christ loved them, that he died for them, that he rose again and is alive today. All they had to do was believe. BUT, they must first hear."

And hear they did! In February 1954, from a 2,500-watt Army surplus transmitter in Tangier, Spanish-language programs began.

But the vision didn't stop there. Spain was just the beginning.

Soon, additional programs in other languages were added to the broadcast lineup. That led to further opportunities to broadcast from other super-power transmitters in strategic locations to reach listeners throughout Europe – including the Soviet-bloc countries – and the Middle East, Central and South America, Asia and Africa.

To help him lead this burgeoning ministry, Paul Freed prayerfully called upon his father, Ralph Freed, and was so pleased when he said "Yes." The Voice of Tangier steadily grew to become Trans World Radio and now TWR.

The vision – and results – have kept expanding, even exploding. And God opened some unique ministry doors in some rather unlikely places.

"Help me, O Lord my God;

save me according to Your lovingkindness.

And let them know that this is Your hand;

You, Lord, have done it."

– PSALM 109:26-27

3

A Secret Listener Takes the Risk

H E HAD CONQUERED mainland Europe, but the crazed dictator wanted more.

This time, Adolf Hitler would use propaganda to help pave the way for his military machine to conquer North Africa. He had an enormous building started in southern France near Monte Carlo and concocted plans for a super-power transmitter to send a long-wave signal across the Mediterranean Sea, singing the glories of Nazi ideology.

History caught up with Hitler, though, and his million-watt dream never became reality. But in less than two decades following the end of World War II, that same facility would be used to tell Europeans the good news of Jesus Christ in the early days of Trans World Radio. An agreement with commercial station Radio Monte Carlo allowed TWR to proclaim the gospel out of "Hitler's building."

"You meant evil against me, but God meant it for good," Joseph told his brothers (Genesis 50:20). In the same way, God turned the evil purposes of Hitler for good in Monte Carlo, allowing TWR to bring the hope of Jesus Christ to countless listeners across the European continent.

And eventually to a military officer in possibly the most repressive communist stronghold.

ONE OF THE many strengths and beauties of international Christian broadcasting is that it can beam the gospel into regions, countries, villages and homes – and even a 10-by-10-foot office – to which missionaries are unable to travel and meet face-to-face with individuals who need Jesus.

That cramped room was the working office of Berti Dosti, a captain in the Albanian army. He was secretly listening to a 15-minute TWR program from Monte Carlo. If he were to be caught, he'd probably be fired from his job. But he took the risk because he wanted to know about God, who was someone the government had tried to ban the Albanian people from knowing about, let alone from following.

By design, Albania was isolated from the rest of the world. After seizing power shortly before the end of World War II, Enver Hoxha ruled the European country – slightly smaller than the state of Maryland – with dictatorial fervor. In fact, he proclaimed Albania to be the world's first atheist country in 1967.

"The fanatical despot waged war on religion just as he had done against the Fascist Italian and German occupiers during the Second World War," journalist and author John Butterworth wrote in *God's Secret Listener*, which chronicles Berti Dosti's amazing story. "He destroyed churches or converted them into post offices, schools, weapon depots, cafes, barns, storehouses or museums. Prison sentences of between three and ten years were imposed for 'religious propaganda' and for the production, distribution or storage of religious literature. Many Orthodox and Catholic priests were sent to prison, tortured and then executed by firing squad."

Dosti, born in April 1957, grew up in a military family. His parents divorced when he was 3 years old. He stayed with his father, an army officer, while his older brother went to live with an aunt. His father eventually remarried.

Religion was never discussed. "My dad was a Communist, and both my parents were atheists," Dosti told TWR in an email interview. "We never heard the word 'God,' and we were not allowed to even say that word."

Electronics fascinated Dosti, and he enjoyed tinkering with radios during his secondary school years. That would bode well for him into the future when he joined the army. He became an officer in 1983. Three years later, at the age of 29, he received the third-highest military medal in the country, recognized for his "distinguished work in organization and leadership in the military base where he served and for attaining very high achievements of practice with his fellow soldiers."

Even when Enver Hoxha died in 1985, Albania remained under the thumb of the Communist Party. Citizens were constantly watched, and the army stood ready to enforce order.

Albania was constantly on high alert, fearing an invasion from the West. "Berti's job, as an expert in radios and communications, was to scan the airwaves for any hint that an enemy was approaching," Butterworth wrote. "Time was spent planning for an invasion and considering how the Albanians should respond."

One night in late 1989, Dosti was scanning the world's airwaves. It was 8:45, and he was halfway through a 24-hour shift. The work was monotonous, and he had grown bored. But he perked up when he heard a voice saying, "If you want to find out more about God, we will meet again next week."

The program was part of a strategic outreach by the European Christian Mission (ECM). Since Albania was closed to any foreign visitors, ECM believed radio was the most effective way to proclaim the gospel to Albania – as well as to Soviet-bloc countries. It recorded the programs in England and sent them to TWR in Monte Carlo, which in turn aired the broadcasts toward Albania. The host was Sali Rahmani, aka Luan Mateu. He had been broadcasting messages to Albania since 1973, not knowing if anybody was listening to his *Way of Peace* program.

Intrigued, Dosti wanted to listen again. But were the risks of satisfying his curiosity worth it? It wouldn't be just him who would be affected if he was caught. What might also happen to his wife Tatjana and their 7-year-old daughter and 2-year-old son? He conferred with Tatjana.

"I was worried, but I have always supported Berti and knew he would be very careful," she was quoted in Butterworth's biography of her husband as saying.

Dosti devised what he felt was a fail-safe plan to ensure he would be alone in his office and not be detected listening to TWR's Monte Carlo broadcast. That night's program examined "Who Is God?" As the clock approached 8:45 p.m. – when the program would begin – Dosti checked to make sure the guard on duty was at the entrance to the base. He told him to notify him immediately if any visitors showed up. Then Dosti closed his office door and put on his headphones. His plan worked!

"This was the first time ever for me to hear about the love of Christ and his death and the forgiveness of sins," he told TWR. "This was a new message for me. We had heard about death on the cross, but I understood that it was only for criminals. They talked about God and about a person called Jesus and that he loved us. In our families, all we talked about was the Communist Party and about political things."

Dosti was troubled, though, by the program's signoff. Sali Rahmani encouraged listeners to write to Luan Mateu at P.O. Box 141, Monte Carlo, Monaco. Dosti kept listening to the programs, sometimes even recording them, but he couldn't muster the courage to send a letter for at least another 18 months.

A lot transpired in that year and a half. The Soviet Union collapsed, and protesting crowds in Tirana, Albania's capital, pulled down the large statue of Enver Hoxha in 1991, signifying the death of communism in their country. "When Albania opened and the first missionaries came, that's when I took the courage to write to Monte Carlo," Dosti said.

That initial letter paved the way for Dosti to take part in correspondence courses with TWR staff. They sent him his first Bible, and he studied it faithfully, taking considerable time to answer each question. He started meeting in person with ECM missionary Stephen Bell, who helped disciple him, and he attended an in-country Bible camp with other TWR listeners.

As he grew in his knowledge of the Scriptures, Dosti understood the implications on his life. "I understood that Jesus was my Savior, and I gave my life completely to him on Nov. 17, 1993, to obey him and to follow him. My desire was to serve the Lord and to share his Word with others."

Dosti even started traveling around 20 miles from his hometown of Lushnjë to Fier to study with Bell about how to preach and proclaim the gospel. That led to his first two sermons: on the happiness of a forgiven sinner, based on Psalm 32, and on the old man versus the new man, based on Colossians 1 and 3.

He has transitioned from Capt. Dosti to Pastor Dosti. Today, he's leading the Way of Peace churches in Lushnjë in west-central Albania and in the village of Bitaj, about an hour's drive from Tirana.

"Our church is involved in reaching the community around us," Dosti explained. "We do a lot of evangelizing and also practical development projects for people in need, including the disabled. We want to show our faith in action, practicing it everywhere. We share the good news but also rebuild schools or houses that have been destroyed. We've equipped people to start small businesses so they can earn a daily living. And we've helped our local hospitals and our state institutions."

That type of outreach blew away Matt Bird, chief executive with Cinnamon Network International, in a podcast interview with Dosti. "Albania has moved in the last 30 years from banning Christians and the church to where the local government is calling you to help. That's huge!"

Dosti responded: "Our role in the community is strong. The local government understands the power of churches. We've sat many times at the table with them, and they always invite us to help them with the needs that they have."

When the opportunity arose to produce a radio program, Dosti jumped at it, knowing personally the lasting difference such a broadcast can make. He's been the speaker of *Word of Hope* ministry in Albania, having recorded more than 500 programs. It's now broadcast on local radio stations across the country. And since 2003, he has served as the chairman of the board for TWR Albania.

BUT DOSTI MIGHT never have heard the message if it had not been for the efforts of a young TWR missionary monitoring the signal from Monte Carlo.

Radio crosses borders, but over the years a few entities have tried to block the message of hope coming from TWR transmitters. Their technique is known as "jamming." They broadcast a competing signal on the same frequency as that used by TWR so that TWR's message can't be heard.

Soviet Russia would sometimes try to do that, said Tom Streeter, who joined the staff of TWR in Monte Carlo in 1972 and now lives with his wife, Elly, in North Carolina.

"But they were not very consistent," Streeter added. "Jamming is not widely effective, especially in a large country. Jamming is also relatively expensive. It also gives the impression that you are afraid of the content of the transmissions that you are trying to block out."

None of this deterred the Hoxha-led government of much smaller Albania. Discovering TWR's 15-minute weekly program, their technicians would power up a jamming transmitter each week, tuned to the same frequency and broadcasting noise, Streeter explained. Following standard practice, TWR in Monte Carlo would start playing its "musical identification" five minutes before the start of the broadcast so that their listeners would have something to tune to. But that also would signal the government technicians to turn on their jamming transmitter. Since the TWR signal had to travel 650 miles to Albania, it would be overpowered by the jammer.

"That was when we began to play cat and mouse," Streeter recalled. "I sat in Monte Carlo listening to our ID tune. For me, the signal in Monte Carlo was very strong. But as soon as the jammer began, I could faintly hear their noise in the background. That was when we would retune our transmitter to another nearby frequency that we knew would not interfere with any other broadcasters."

TWR's listeners in Albania learned to retune their radios, finding the gospel broadcast on the new frequency, Streeter said. But for the jammers, their own signal was so loud that they never realized they were no longer blocking the broadcast.

A bored Berti Dosti would one day come across the tail end of one of those broadcasts, and the Holy Spirit would work through that.

"I was thrilled when I first read Berti Dosti's story," Streeter said. "That was when I finally learned that our attempts to outwit the Albanian government jammers had been successful."

LET DOSTI HAVE the last word.

"As Joshua 24:15 says, 'As for me and my family, we will serve the Lord,'" he said. "For us, Christ is everything. He is our life, and we live for him. We are looking forward to meeting Christ in eternity."

The Monte Carlo long-wave transmitter site at Col de la Madone, France, was in use until about 1980.

SECTION II

Riding Waves on Our Knees

MINISTRIES LIKE TWR just don't happen. Far from it. From the outset, those whom God called to TWR started – and continue to start – their days on their knees, praising God for who he is and pouring out their hearts to him for his wisdom, grace and power. They begin their mornings scouring the Scriptures, asking the Lord to speak to their hearts and to transform their lives to be more like Jesus. They want to please him! And they conclude their days with praise and thanksgiving, for his faithfulness.

God has honored their faith. He has answered their prayers. Always in his perfect timing. Now, that has often meant TWR missionaries and staff have had to wait upon the Lord. But God has always met their needs, whether it be for people, resources, equipment – whatever! Sometimes, it's been miraculous. And always marvelous. So that he, and he alone, gets the glory!

"For the needy will not always be forgotten nor the hope of the afflicted perish forever."

— PSALM 9:18

4

Caribbean Miracles

WITH HER OLD Russian radio in her time-weathered hands, Josephina stood next to the big aluminum pot on her stove. She kept pacing around and checking the radio dial. The 94-year-old blind Cuban woman was desperately trying to locate the best signal for TWR's programming emanating from the tiny Caribbean island of Bonaire about 1,000 miles away near the northern coast of Venezuela.

The aluminum pot would pull in the signal and then be coupled with the radio receiver.

Josephina was hosting a small yet enthusiastic group of listeners at her home in a village west of Havana. She had been listening to TWR since its AM station first signed on in 1964. She especially loved the programs for children. Her favorite was *Pedrito el Pulpo (Little Peter the Octopus)*, produced by TWR Venezuela and featuring dramatized stories with biblical and ethical applications woven in.

"I don't ever want to miss any of them," Josephina said.

One of the guests in her home that night in 2011 was Joe Barker, then station director for 800 AM on Bonaire. Barker was in Cuba assessing the impact of technological issues affecting TWR's signal toward Cuba. During his trip, he met with listeners, like Josephina and her friends, to hear how they depended on TWR programming for their spiritual growth.

Barker was amazed by what he saw. "Why do you stand up, Josephina? Couldn't you get a chair and sit down, something like that?"

"Oh no, no, no," she replied. "I stand up so that if I fall asleep, I'll fall over and wake up, so I don't miss anything."

Barker shook his head in wonder, astounded at her faithful commitment. He took her picture and displayed it in TWR's break room at the Bonaire station.

"Every morning before prayer for the day or at other times when things got tough, our staff would look at Josephina's photo and remind ourselves who benefits from our daily work," Barker said. "She came to represent all of our audience members because it reminded us that our work wasn't just for a number of nameless, faceless people but that it was for a large number of individual people who have a personal connection and vested interest in our work."

TOUGH, FAITH-CHALLENGING QUESTIONS have certainly come to the forefront over the decades with the operation on Bonaire – such as issues that necessitated dispatching Barker to research the signal dilemma affecting the ministry's outreach to Cuba.

About 10 years following TWR's founding in 1954, interest turned to determining how to help reach Central and South America with the gospel of Jesus Christ. TWR's leaders initially researched the possible launching of a ministry from the Caribbean island of Curaçao. Government officials there eagerly explored the prospect with founder Dr. Paul Freed. Negotiations were sailing along. But a fateful discovery torpedoed the plan. The station's location would be too close to the island's jet airport, posing problems both for TWR's radio signal and for incoming jets.

Hearts sank. But God broke through the cloud of disappointment and opened the door for a grand, and an even more ideal, solution on the nearby island of Bonaire. It is a special municipality – a public body – of the Netherlands. Upon invitation from the island's lieutenant governor, TWR's leadership team investigated the new location. Excitement was rekindled. "There were fewer people on Bonaire than Curaçao. There was no jet airport," Dr. Freed wrote in *Towers to Eternity*. "And the large salt flats gave us conditions that appeared to be technically superior." God knew, and he provided!

Broadcasts began in August 1964. The 500,000-watt Continental transmitter was said to be the most powerful AM transmitter in the Western Hemisphere, its AM signal so strong it reached far into Canada and all the way down to Tierra del Fuego in Argentina. But the primary focus was Cuba, Colombia, Venezuela and northern Brazil.

Soon letters and reports flooded TWR's office. People described giving their hearts to Jesus and how their lives were no longer the same as they gobbled up the Bible-centric programs.

That original transmitter in time wore out and was replaced by a 500,000-watt Brown Boveri Corp. transmitter. But in 1999, its tubes began showing signs they were nearing the end of their life cycle, and that's when TWR leaders were confronted with a vexing quandary. One of those tubes alone cost $150,000. And the price of diesel fuel to run everything was soaring.

"We had to decide whether it was a really good idea to invest large sums of money in operating this transmitter – an old, tube-based, water-cooled, inefficiently designed system, which was good for its day, but that had fallen behind the times," Joe Barker explained.

"The choice was made to focus not so much on a huge geographic area but on unserved and underserved areas that were closer to Bonaire," he said.

A 100,000-watt, solid-state Nautel transmitter was selected, and new towers and antenna system were erected. But that decision was not universally embraced. "Initially, a lot of our partners expressed their disappointment at the decrease of our power level," Barker said. "But over time, new listeners still found us in southeastern Cuba and across the

Caribbean and into Venezuela and portions of Brazil."

Then out of left field – soon after Lauren Libby became president and chief executive officer in late 2008 – a major bombshell dropped, sending reverberations throughout the region. Regulating authorities on Bonaire told TWR it would be limited to 50,000 watts at night. And they were not open for discussion, let alone negotiation.

That would only aggravate the situation, for some listeners in hard-to-reach areas of Cuba were still voicing their worries that they couldn't hear the programs with regularity because the 100,000-watt signal was weak – or worse, that it couldn't be picked up at all.

To say the least, spirits at the Bonaire station had essentially hit rock bottom. In 2009, one of Libby's first trips as the new president was to the island, along with Chief Development Officer Tim Klingbeil. They wanted to assess the operation in person. They were stunned.

Because of all the transmitter downgrades that had been made, a significant number of staff positions had been eliminated. Only a handful remained – a skeleton of what it once was. They included Barker, Program Director Brad Swanson, an administrator and a couple of Bonaire locals who worked at the station.

"We were just about ready to close the doors, to be honest," Libby said. "At one point, Tim and I looked at each other and I said, 'What would it take to bring this back online possibly up to 500,000 watts as we had in the beginning?'"

Klingbeil replied, "It's going to take a lot of money, and it will take a rebuild."

They, and the Bonaire team, collectively gulped. At the same time, though, they were re-energized, imagining what God could do.

PRAYER WAS CRITICAL to handling this barrage of challenges. Alerts were sent around the world. The more people prayed – and the more TWR leadership sought God's will – the more they became convinced that TWR needed to boost Bonaire's signal.

"Lauren had this God-given vision that we needed to increase the power again from Bonaire," Klingbeil said. "The people who were living in those areas affected by the loss of power were saying, 'We need that power and signal back.' Our leadership believed we needed to again be a powerful influence in Latin America."

Joe Barker's trip to Cuba confirmed that need. With a more powerful transmitter and an amplified signal, he believed TWR could reach more listeners like Josephina and her home-study friends.

Proverbs 21:1 became a key Bible verse and promise: "The king's heart is like channels of water in the hand of the Lord; He turns it wherever He pleases."

God heard the prayers of his people. As Barker talked up front with whatever officials on Bonaire would listen, the Holy Spirit was at work behind the scenes changing attitudes and overseeing future directives. "One day, we were told that we were going to have our power level restricted to 50,000 watts at night, and the next day we received permission to return to 450,000 watts of power," Barker said.

Alberto González Muñoz (in the front, at right), the Cuban voice for TWR, speaks to a gathering at a church in the Cuban city of Camaguey.

He immediately called Libby and Klingbeil and, before long, the board of directors got excited. But Barker gasped.

"At that particular time, there were only five staff on Bonaire, and one of them was part time," he said. "We at one time had more than 50. So how could the five of us rebuild a whole new facility and keep this one on the air at the same time?"

Barker had to look no farther than his workstation for comfort – and for the spiritual answer. There, on the recommendation of a pastor friend, he had taped James 1:5 to his computer monitor: "If any of you lacks wisdom, let him ask of God, who gives to all generously and without reproach, and it will be given to him."

When the board approved ramping up the signal and purchasing a 450,000-watt Nautel transmitter, Barker was at peace that God would provide the equipment, the funds and the people to get the job done.

When fundraising began in 2014, the Bonaire Transmitter Power Up Project was tied to both TWR's 60th anniversary and Bonaire's 50th anniversary. The goal was $3.8 million.

"That was a hefty, monumental goal," Klingbeil said. "It was pretty scary because of its size."

The first gift came from a radio station 9,468 miles away in Papua New Guinea. Wantok Radio Light, a network of 25 FM stations and a shortwave station, broadcasts Christian teaching and music 24 hours a day. Their donation of 10,000 kina – approximately US$2,850 – was given in partnership with Life Radio Ministries of Atlanta, Georgia. A note attached to their gift read, "We are island people, and we want to reach island people."

"They heard about the need to reach Cuba, and they wanted to participate in it," Klingbeil said.

The project elicited donations from across the globe, a major feat indeed. The Christian broadcasting community in the U.S. got behind the project. Northwestern Radio, one of 50 local stations and nationwide networks that took part in the campaign, contributed a sizable donation.

A large gift came from a soybean farmer in Brazil. One of his many farms is the size of Rhode Island. Another significant gift came from a family and their foundation in Pennsylvania, connected with project coordinators Daryl and Carol VanDyken. All kinds, all sizes. God, once again, showed his glory!

Over the years it took to complete the project, well over 200 volunteers traveled to Bonaire to assist with the upgrade. Engineers. Electricians. Experts in air conditioning. Project managers.

Among them was a group of eight people from a Methodist church in Houston, recruited by John, its missions pastor. They went down and helped rebuild some of the antenna systems. Undoubtedly, God used John as a catalyst to begin to move things forward.

Libby also recalls visiting a church in Topeka, Kansas. He attended a Sunday-school class where longtime friends David and Suzanne Osborne are members. Libby was asked to talk about the Bonaire project. Afterward, Dave, a local contractor who has since passed away, asked what materials were needed. Copper to put inside the antenna matching system at the base of each tower, Libby said.

Technician Art Thompson checks the equipment during the early days of the Bonaire Transmitter, in the early 1960s.

"How much will that cost?" Dave asked.

"Probably $70,000 to $80,000," Libby said.

Dave then challenged the class. "I'm going to stand at the door and take pledges, and I want $70,000," Dave told the group. "Not only that, I want about 15 of you to go to Bonaire with me to install it."

Close to $50,000 was pledged that morning. But $70,000 ended up coming in! So the copper was bought and shipped to Bonaire.

And a group of 15 traveled to the Caribbean island and refurbished each one of the matching units on the four towers. "This was spiritual entrepreneurship again in action," Libby noted.

But the Bonaire upgrade campaign didn't attract attention just within the United States. The ministry's global family contributed toward its success. Lemuel Larrosa, then TWR's director of Hispanic Ministry, stood up at a national partners conference and declared, "This is not just a North American project. It's also a South American and a Latin American project." At the same time, TWR's partner in the Netherlands especially got behind it. "It gave heavily to Bonaire since Bonaireans are part of the Netherlands," Libby said. "That was another wonderful example of how God moved in the hearts of people."

On June 16, 2017, the funding goal had been met. The staff praised the Lord and thanked everyone across the globe who helped make this happen. Through many combined efforts, God supplied TWR's need, and the ministry decided to celebrate his goodness publicly.

TWR friends and family, local guests and dignitaries gathered on Bonaire on Jan. 30, 2018, to formally dedicate the upgraded radio station. Its expanded ministry reach across the region is bringing sound gospel programming to roughly 100 million potential listeners.

And the signal to Cuba? Whereas before it was received mainly in the south and sporadically elsewhere, it's now blanketing the entire island nation. God clearly guided – and continues to bless – TWR's long-term plans!

"You are the God who works wonders;
You have made known Your strength
among the peoples."

— PSALM 77:14

5

Tiny Nation, Big Pulpit

IT MADE NO sense, Sphiwe Nxumalo-Ngwenya thought.

Growing up in the nation then known as Swaziland, she would hear her country described as the "pulpit" of Africa. But her homeland, now called Eswatini, was so small. If she thought of it in terms of a map of the United States, it would be a little smaller than New Jersey. More likely, she thought of it in terms of African nations that dwarfed Eswatini, including neighboring countries South Africa and Mozambique.

In such a huge continent, how would anyone pay attention to little Swaziland? It was akin to Nathanael saying, "Can anything good come out of Nazareth?" (John 1:46).

It was not until 2015, when she was a grown woman who had joined TWR, that Nxumalo-Ngwenya understood.

"Indeed, we are reaching quite a wide area through TWR's broadcasts from the tiny kingdom in the bushes," she said more recently. "You would not know that something so big in reaching the world is happening."

Eswatini can be called the pulpit of Africa because the little kingdom was the first in Africa where TWR was able to plant a transmitting site. It gave, and still gives, Eswatini a gospel impact that goes far beyond its borders.

"When God opened the transmission site, we were able to reach most of the continent of Africa via high-power shortwave broadcasting from the country of Eswatini," said Lauren Libby, president of TWR.

It started with what is known in TWR lore as the miracle of the sandbar.

FOR A TIME, it appeared that TWR's first transmitter in Africa would be in Swaziland's much larger next-door neighbor.

As longtime TWR missionary Bill Mial recounted in the TWR memoir *Great Things He Has Done*, TWR turned to Swaziland when the South African Broadcast Corp. (SABC) balked at allowing what it saw as competition into the country. The South African government overruled the SABC's objections, paving the way for TWR to locate there. Later, though, the government abruptly reversed its call, so it was back to Swaziland to build a new station.

TWR found a site near Manzini, Swaziland's largest city. Mial was based in Monte Carlo for TWR at the time. But he was responsible for the African project, so he made frequent visits to Swaziland and South Africa. When he saw the site, he said, he was excited to see that a little stream ran through the property.

That was on a Friday. Over the weekend, upstream storms transformed the creek into a raging torrent. When Mial returned on Monday, it already had receded somewhat, but grass hanging from trees marked how high the water had risen.

"It was impressive," Mial recalled almost five decades later. "And I thought, 'Oh, so much for the cute little creek,' you know? And then we had the challenge of how do we get to work, because we were building the transmitter building on one side of the creek, and the road came into the property on the other side."

Bridges were built, but floods washed them away, Mial remembered. Eventually, a "swinging bridge" was erected so people could cross on foot during floods.

Construction on the transmitter building went ahead, but the contractors needed a certain kind of sand that wasn't available on-site. TWR missionary Larry McGuire, who served in Swaziland at that time, picked up the story for the 40th anniversary celebration in 2014.

"In 1973 and '74, during the early stages of construction, we were taking sand from beside the river near the end of the current suspension bridge," McGuire wrote. "The sand was being used to make thousands of concrete blocks, and to pour foundations and anchors for buildings and antennas.

"Maybe 30% of the way into the project, we had nearly used up all the available sand. We were investigating the logistics and were overwhelmed by the cost of purchasing and transporting hundreds of tons of sand to continue the construction.

"About then, we experienced some very heavy rains. Since this was before the roads and building site were graveled, the roads and working conditions became extremely muddy. ... When the river receded, the sand that we had used up had been replaced, plus more – a whole lot more!

TOP LEFT: Motorists cross a bridge at the Swaziland transmitter site in the 1970s. A storm briefly turned the stream seen here into a raging torrent, but it left behind a gift of sand that was perfect for construction purposes. **TOP RIGHT:** Bill Mial (pictured in 2013) led the effort to establish TWR's fourth transmitter in Swaziland (now Eswatini).

So, while we were fretting, God was providing – abundantly!"

It was one of four incidents McGuire cited "that reflect how God answered a need before we even knew to ask," he said.

When it began broadcasting on Nov. 1, 1974, the Swaziland transmitting site became TWR's fourth, after Monte Carlo, Bonaire and Cyprus. The Swazi government granted approval for the project in June 1973, and God supplied the four transmitters used in the beginning. The original purpose of these World War II-era transmitters isn't known, but in any event, they hadn't been used. Nor had they been used by a U.S. farmer with a passion for radio who bought them at an auction after the war. When the farmer learned that TWR was building a station in Africa, he donated the transmitters.

Along the way, TWR engineers didn't hesitate to repurpose transmitters to affordably keep the Swaziland signals alive and thriving. In March 1981, TWR Swaziland had its first AM broadcasts to southern Africa via a 50,000-watt transmitter with a curious history. In the 1960s, when only the BBC was licensed to serve England, several "pirate" radio stations operated from offshore ships. Since they were in international waters, the British government couldn't stop them. But legislation passed in 1967 made it much more difficult for the pirate stations to make money. The result was failed stations with surplus equipment. According to a 2016 video made in Swaziland, TWR was able to buy a transmitter from one of the pirate stations at an auction in the 1970s for a bargain price.

Still later, one of four transmitters that Werner Kroemer, then TWR international vice president of operations, found at a bargain price in Germany was shipped to Swaziland and installed at the site, McGuire said. After the antenna tuning system was upgraded, the AM transmitter was brought up from 50,000 watts to 100,000 watts.

THE STATION, WHICH is celebrating its 50th anniversary in 2024, has seen significant changes in that time. Even the name of the country has changed; it became Eswatini by royal decree in April 2018.

The setting for the Eswatini transmitting site is idyllic, but torrential downpours can cause sudden changes.

Today, TWR has three 100,000-watt shortwave transmitters and the one 100,000-watt AM transmitter in Eswatini, said Steve Stavropoulos, who was the longtime chief engineer there. Shortwave coverage includes Zimbabwe and Malawi in southern Africa; the Democratic Republic of Congo and Burundi in Central Africa; Kenya, Uganda, Tanzania, Mozambique and Madagascar in East Africa; and Ethiopia, Eritrea and Somalia in the Horn of Africa. The AM transmitter reaches South Africa and Zimbabwe.

Serving at the Eswatini station isn't for the faint of heart, said Juliet Oppong-Amoako, who as media services director for Africa is the point person for shaping TWR media strategy on the continent. The staff are in the "middle of nowhere" and deal routinely with challenges such as contending with black mambas, the world's second-longest venomous snake. In the 2016 video, Stavropoulos described sticking his head even with an above-ground platform, only to come face-to-face with a black mamba. He made a quick exit.

"These are the tough conditions they live in, but they have a reason to wake up every morning to make sure that our broadcasts go out and go out problem-free," Oppong-Amoako said.

Their audience appreciates it. Among Eswatini listeners to *Thru the Bible* in the Zulu language, one said his marriage was saved, a single mother said she learned to speak positively to her teenage sons and a young man said he realized he needed to forgive his father, all from what they heard on the program.

Eswatini, the last absolute monarchy in Africa, has proven to be the ideal place for TWR because it has not been afflicted by the conflicts so common elsewhere on the continent, Stavropoulos said.

"There's hardly a country in Africa that TWR could have operated in for 50 years in a peaceful situation," Stavropoulos said during a 2022 interview. "We've been very blessed in this country to have that stability."

Libby highlighted TWR's warm, long-standing relationship with the king and government of Eswatini.

"But God is the one who opened the door as we moved into a situation where we were looking for a place to talk to Africa," he said. "Then God opened the door in Eswatini."

Section II: Riding Waves on Our Knees

"By awesome deeds You answer us in righteousness,

God of our salvation, You who are the trust of all

the ends of the earth and the farthest sea."

– PSALM 65:5

6

Through Storms, Building a Secure Future on Guam

G RAB MY LUGGAGE *and head home,* TWR President Lauren Libby thought after his long business trip. Simple enough. Routine enough.

Not this day. God would reveal something extraordinary in the baggage claim area in Raleigh-Durham International Airport. Something remarkable he didn't anticipate.

While Libby waited for his bags, four young men were off-loading their equipment. Their physiques arrested his attention, as did their attire. "They were rather hefty, strong, muscular guys," he remembered. "And they had 'Tower Crew' emblazoned on their T-shirts."

Libby's antenna quickly went up. TWR had lined up an overseas company to tackle a major tower restoration project on the Pacific island of Guam. They were well known for their expert maintenance of shortwave broadcast towers and antennas in other locations. But at the last minute, their riggers couldn't travel to the U.S. territory because of strict COVID-19 restrictions then in place.

That was a huge disappointment because TWR was racing against the clock as salty air, humidity and rust were wreaking havoc on those 10 towers. Installed when TWR began broadcasting via shortwave to Asia in January 1977, they had outlived their life expectancy. The fear was that a Pacific typhoon that can reach 200 miles per hour could threaten the massive tower and curtain-antenna infrastructure and cause a catastrophic interruption of ministry. Dead airtime could spell disaster.

Back to square one, TWR's leaders were at a loss as to who could then handle the project to rehabilitate and refurbish the aging towers.

"What do you guys do?" Libby asked the group.

"We just got back from erecting towers in the Caribbean," they replied.

"Interesting. We put up a lot of towers," Libby answered.

"Oh yeah?"

"All over the world."

The tower group were now intrigued. They struck up a conversation with Libby, who got their phone number. It just so happened that the company was located about a half-hour away from TWR's U.S. office – completely under the radar!

Their contact info was passed on to Joe Barker, TWR's chief technology officer, who immediately contacted them. "I went over and talked with them about the Guam project," Barker said. "I asked them if they could come and look at the towers and see if they'd be interested in the project."

Before long, the company's owner flew to the island – 3,945 miles west of Hawaii and 1,623 miles south of Japan – to investigate and assess the situation. He climbed up and down the 370-foot towers with TWR's on-site team and reported back: "We can do this. We can help you."

What great news.

"That was not mere happenstance," Libby said. "I didn't just meet those guys at baggage claim out of the clear, blue sky. No, that was God's faithfulness again on display."

The Lord answered prayer. An unforgettable moment in time!

God's providence would again be monumentally revealed soon after this restoration commenced.

"PERFORMING THIS TOWER restoration project is essential to the long-term future of TWR broadcasting from Guam," said Darin Alvord, who has been serving as volunteer project manager, working closely with the North Carolina firm.

Alvord came to TWR with extensive experience overseeing tower construction, installation and maintenance. He had sold his business and retired and was seeking God's will for his next chapter. That's when he discovered the need for a project manager for the tower restoration project at the Guam station KTWR. God led him and his wife, Linda, to the Pacific island.

"Restoring these mighty towers is a part of the effort needed to continue broadcasting for the next two or more decades," he said. "The importance of shortwave radio in transmitting hope, blessings and instruction to millions and millions of people – blocked from the truth otherwise and who need the truth of the gospel – cannot be overstated."

For more than four decades, God has been using the broadcasts from KTWR to reach and change lives throughout the vast Asian continent. Listeners live in such diverse places as China, North Korea, Vietnam, Laos, Myanmar, Indonesia, India, Taiwan, Thailand, Mongolia and Japan. And when brutal fighting erupted in Ukraine in 2022, cutting off some of TWR's usual outlets for broadcasting to that region, TWR was able to beam hope-filled programming from Guam to war-ravaged areas over 6,000 miles away.

An immense and intense spiritual battle is being waged for the hearts of Asia's some 4 billion people. The Christian faith is oftentimes dwarfed by other major world religions. In several countries, proclaiming the gospel of Jesus Christ is restricted, if not forbidden. It can be impossible or extremely challenging to start churches or carry out on-the-ground evangelism and discipleship. Persecution is real for many believers.

KTWR's programming, offered in 27 languages, is therefore vital to advancing God's kingdom and fulfilling Christ's Great Commission to go and make disciples of all nations. Shortwave has the power to travel long distances, crossing geographical, ideological, political and religious barriers and reaching into peoples' homes and hearts with the message of the gospel.

Some broadcasters in recent years, including Christian ministries, began to question the long-term validity and viability of shortwave. A few of them even shut down their sites, thinking they could provide content more reliably and cheaper over the internet. Since restrictions at the time were far looser in places like China, they wondered, "Why not shift away from shortwave?" That approach ended up being shortsighted, to their peril.

TWR, on the other hand, thought otherwise. In fact, the ministry increased its shortwave content.

At the same time, more and more Asian countries were transitioning to digital broadcasting, a popular growing market. So TWR started working closely with two manufacturers of receivers based on Digital Radio Mondiale technology with the goal of disseminating more of them in Asia.

That latest technology, combined with its continued analog shortwave broadcasts, positioned TWR to respond as the circumstances dictated.

That's certainly been the case in China when authorities clamped down on Christian media and on evangelism. They censored Christian content and tracked internet activity. Churches closed, crosses were bulldozed, and pastors were beaten and imprisoned. Persecution was once more on the rise.

TWR staff quickly mobilized a response. They added more *Discipleship on the Air* programs. They began airing a new program titled *Following Jesus*, produced by the International Mission Board, which incorporates drama and Bible storytelling to challenge non-Christians. And *Mission 66*, a study of all 66 books of the Bible, was added to the broadcast lineup. All of these are offered in Mandarin.

The impact was immediate. "The *Mission 66* program was very helpful to me," one listener wrote from Beijing. "The content healed my depression and helped me find meaning and value in life. I hope more people will hear it."

From its station on the island of Guam with the power of shortwave, TWR can reach a large swath of Asia, including North Korea and parts of China and India.

TWR'S BOARD OF directors approved the tower restoration project in the fall of 2020, and the fundraising and prayer campaign began in January 2021, adopting Proverbs 18:10 as its theme verse: "The name of the Lord is a strong tower; The righteous runs into it and is safe."

"With all of our projects, we put together our best plans, but God always provides, usually in unexpected and unplanned ways," said Tim Klingbeil, TWR's chief development officer.

With the initial restoration project, one gift totaling $250,000 came in without any fanfare. It was from a donor in the Midwest who had heard about the project over Christian radio, through a TWR fundraising letter and from the ministry's magazine.

"This was the biggest gift he had ever given in his life," Klingbeil explained. "He's not married, and he took it out of his retirement savings. He told us, 'I have plenty of money since I've been saving for the last 40 years. I'm very frugal.'"

By the end of 2022, work was well underway. On tap to be replaced were 2,500 braces, 110 ladders and guy wires. "The company's riggers are very, very hard workers, sometimes on the towers up to 10 hours per day, six days a week," Barker said. "We're extremely pleased with their work."

That phase of the project was scheduled to be completed in 2023. But it was interrupted – dramatically.

IN LATE MAY 2023, Super Typhoon Mawar barreled through the Pacific and crashed into Guam with sustained 140 mph winds. But praise the Lord, his providential hand was once more evident.

Things could have been much worse because at the last minute, the powerful storm skirted north, avoiding a bull's-eye landing. If it had remained on course and struck the KTWR station at full force, the damage could have been catastrophic.

Miraculously, the typhoon claimed no lives on Guam. But KTWR's five curtain antennas received varying levels of damage, and the station's gospel broadcasts across Asia were off the air. Staff families, as did other Guam residents, struggled with power cuts and water outages as Mawar disrupted island life. Yet they persevered and labored on.

Other shortwave broadcasters were contracted to carry portions of the radio programming until KTWR staff – in what their ministry colleagues considered a supernaturally blessed superhuman effort – made repairs and gradually brought the antennas online. As of July 15, 2023, the station was beaming its full broadcast schedule to Asia once again.

"I want to express sincere thanks to all ministry partners who held TWR's Guam team up in prayer and financially supported the repair and recovery work," wrote Daryl Renshaw, TWR's vice president for Asia and coordinator of the global recovery effort.

More than 2,000 missions-minded supporters stepped forward in the middle of the crisis to help underwrite the costly repairs – giving more than $550,000!

"Our team members could not have done what they did without the relentless prayers and sacrificial giving that began quickly after we made the station's needs known," Renshaw added. "TWR's ministry partners' faithfulness has enabled us to resume broadcast ministry to countless people who rely on our nightly broadcasts. I pray that God will richly bless each person who responded to TWR's appeal."

Super Typhoon Mawar made a mess of TWR's antennas on Guam in May 2023. TWR's Mike Lambert (from left) and Travis Herwy and Dalton Ragsdale of contractor Banner Enterprises were among those who worked heroically to get the station back to a full schedule by mid-July 2023.

Listeners, many of whom count on TWR as their primary source of Bible teaching and encouragement, expressed their thank-yous to the Guam staff – and to TWR friends worldwide.

"The broadcast on KTWR has finally returned," one listener said. "I feel so happy! I can listen to the programs on our radio station again every night, and this makes my life more fulfilling."

Another wrote: "Thank you very much for doing your best to restore the transmission facilities and antennas in this difficult situation. *KTWR Friendship Radio* is one of my favorite broadcasts. I would like to sincerely thank you for the early restoration."

PRAISE GOD, MINISTRY continues from Guam. But the destructive storm did halt work on the original Strong Tower for Asia restoration project. But there's good news on that front. The North Carolina contractor's crew was scheduled to come back in 2024 to complete it.

"Typhoon Mawar, combined with Guam's rainy season, which begins in July, together prevented further work on the project until the dry season returns in January 2024," said Darin Alvord.

May God's grace once again prevail.

"The Mighty One, God, the Lord,

has spoken and summoned the earth,

from the rising of the sun to its setting."

— PSALM 50:1 NASB

7

Seed Planters in Japan's Hard Soil

IT WAS AT a packed stadium in Singapore that Samuel Tan saw how many shared his heart for Japan. The year was 2018, and more than 50,000 people were gathered for a prayer conference sponsored by a group called Love Singapore, said Tan, who at the time was TWR's Northeast Asia director.

A huge map of the globe was drawn on the stadium's field, and the speaker called for attendees to come and stand in the part of the globe they felt the Holy Spirit was leading them to. Who is called for Africa? Who is called for China?

"But the moment he mentioned Japan – wow!" Tan recalled. "You see the rush of the people to stand on the map of Japan."

Singapore loves Japan; Asia loves Japan; and most significantly, Jesus loves Japan. But the Land of the Rising Sun has traditionally been seen as hard soil for the gospel.

"Unlike other countries, there is no visible persecution now in Japan," said Hirotaka Sasaki, TWR Japan national leader. "However, I feel that there is an impression that no matter how many seeds of the gospel we sow, they do not bear fruit."

THE JAPANESE PEOPLE see Christianity as incompatible with their culture, said Tan, who led TWR Northeast Asia from 2012-2021.

"When you uphold something as more important than God, it becomes an idol," Samuel Tan said. "This is the stronghold. If anyone challenges the Japanese culture, [the Japanese] will not let go."

Aaron Tan, who is no relation to Samuel but succeeded him as the Northeast Asia director and now serves as TWR vice president for Asia, said cultic activities in recent decades seem to have increased the wariness of Japanese people about any form of religion. Those include the 1995 sarin gas attack on the Tokyo subway system by members of a cult and the assassination of former Prime Minister Shinzo Abe by someone who believed Abe had links to the Unification Church.

"Hence, the Japanese people may tar all churches with the same brush, including mainstream evangelical churches," Aaron Tan said.

The numbers bear that out. According to the Christian research initiative Joshua Project, fewer than 1 in 200 of the Japanese people in Japan are evangelical believers. The four main islands of Japan include more than 8,000 Christian churches. But many of them are very small, said Jonathan Chen, Japan ministry mobilizer for TWR, having fewer than 10 members.

YET SOMETHING SEEMED to change after March 11, 2011, said Pastor Park Sang Bum, TWR Asia's Japan ministry director. That was the date of the Tōhoku tsunami and earthquake on the island of Honshu that killed as many as 18,500 people, left more than 450,000 people homeless and sparked a major disaster at the Fukushima nuclear power plant. It was said to be the most expensive natural disaster in Japan's history.

"After the tsunami, after the disaster in Japan, many people softened their hearts," Park said.

"It was interesting to see how God used that," Libby said.

TWR already had been broadcasting to Japan via shortwave from the island of Guam, Samuel Tan said. Previously, TWR Asia sought to add programming on commercial FM stations, but they had shown no interest. After the tsunami, TWR produced a program in response to the despair left by the disaster. It was called *Season of Hope* and was eagerly welcomed by two FM stations in the Tōhoku area, which began carrying it in 2013.

That network had grown by 2023 to 29 commercial FM stations carrying as many as five TWR programs. Among them were broadcasts of *Women of Hope* and *Every Man A Warrior.*

When Samuel Tan began his assignment in 2012, one of his priorities was Japan. He sensed a need to supplement TWR's mass media outreach with on-the-ground ministry. He settled on what might seem like an old-fashioned approach: distributing tracts.

Japanese people walk from a Shinto shrine in Tokyo. Most Japanese people embrace Shinto – the native religion of Japan – and Buddhism.

Samuel Tan called it "donkey tracting," the name inspired by Zechariah 9:9, which concludes: "Behold, your king is coming to you; righteous and having salvation is he; humble and mounted on a donkey, on a colt, the foal of a donkey."

In a donkey-tracting mission, short-term missionaries join with members of Japanese churches to saturate an area, distributing gospel tracts, radio program fliers and information about local churches. From 2014 through 2023, 28 donkey-tracting missions had taken place in partnership with 115 local Japanese churches and involving about 300 individuals. Three more were scheduled for 2024.

Chen, who led the first of four 2023 missions, said Japanese churches can feel isolated. "So to have people from another country come and visit and serve together alongside them is really a big deal for them. And quite eye-opening as well. ... For the first time, they mentioned, they really are part of the Church – this big body of Christ."

ANOTHER SIGNIFICANT OUTREACH in Japan for TWR is in the area of men's ministry.

TWR's Every Man A Warrior has grown quickly in Japan.

"That's the power of media," Libby said. "That's the power of using broadcasts, printed materials and small groups all coming together. It's very, very powerful. It's very movement-oriented, and God uses that to not only raise up leadership but also to affect future generations."

ALSO IN 2023, Chen was beginning to develop a TWR strategy for a particular subset in the Japanese culture: the hikikomori. This is a Japanese term referring to people who are socially withdrawn. According to the Japanese government, an individual has to be isolated in his or her room for six months or longer to be considered hikikomori, Chen said.

This phenomenon goes much deeper than 20-year-old males obsessed with video games. "Many of them, yeah, maybe they started when

Shuji Kondo records a program in Japanese from KTWR in Guam in 1980. Although Japan is seen as "hard soil," TWR Asian ministry directors have noticed a softening since the 2011 tsunami and earthquake.

they were in their 20s or 30s," Chen said. "But over time they've stayed in this state for 10 years or more, so they are in their 40s or 50s and still being supported by their elderly parents, who may be in their 70s or 80s."

As a media ministry, TWR is well-placed to reach out to the hikikomori because many of them spend time online, he said.

"Media is the only source of interaction with the world outside their room, so we have a means of reaching them in that sense," Chen said. "Many of them also have no sense of purpose or something meaningful to work with. So we can share with them that there is hope, meaning in the gospel."

Of course, hikikomori will need one-on-one counseling to emerge from their isolation, Chen said. But through media, TWR can be a bridge to connect appropriate ministries with the hikikomori.

AS JAPANESE HEARTS perhaps have softened toward the gospel, hearts in the rest of Asia have softened toward Japan, Samuel Tan said. For a long time, it was difficult to find much sympathy for Japan in the rest of Asia – even among Christians – because of leftover bitterness stemming from World War II. "Now the situation has changed. ... I think that season is over."

Now, Singaporeans and others enjoy going to Japan because it's a safe, clean country with polite people and wonderful food, Samuel Tan said. "People like to go because it's such a beautiful people group."

Even if the numbers aren't yet great, Japanese people do respond to the message of hope.

"When I was in high school, I used to listen to KTWR's shortwave broadcasts from the island of Guam," a current listener to TWR's FM programs wrote. "I stopped listening to it when I became a working adult and no longer had time. I was a seeker at the time, and I was baptized at the age of 20. I am now 60 years old. If I hadn't listened to it, I wouldn't have met the Lord."

When thinking of the spiritual state of Japan, Park said he's mindful of the account in 1 Kings 18 of the prophet Elijah sending his servant seven times to see if rain was coming. The seventh time, the servant saw "a little cloud like a man's hand rising from the sea." That cloud soon became a deluge.

"In Japan, we still have a small cloud only," Park said. "But our God doesn't give up."

"My soul, wait in silence for God only,

for my hope is from Him.

He only is my rock and my salvation,

my stronghold; I shall not be shaken."

— PSALM 62:5-6

8

Hope in a Cuban Sugar-Cane Field

WITH A GLEAMING smile on his face, Alberto González Muñoz helped cut the ribbon at the 2018 dedication ceremony of the new transmitter at TWR's station on Bonaire. His presence and integral participation were only fitting since TWR had played such a pivotal role in his own life and Christian experience.

But ministry was the furthest thing from Alberto's mind while growing up in Cuba. As a young boy, he had two grand ambitions. His vocational goal was to become an architect. And he wanted to live out that dream in the United States.

God, however, would take him in a far different direction.

Alberto grew up in a middle-class family in Cárdenas City on Cuba's northern shoreline. His grandparents were faithful Christians and served as deacons at their church. His mother was also a believer. He gave his heart to Jesus after hearing the gospel at church when he was 9 years old.

On his 11th birthday, he wrote to Standard Oil of New Jersey, which at that time was marketing its products under the brand name Esso (the phonetic pronunciation of the initials 'S' and 'O' in Standard Oil). It was mailing maps of the U.S. to anyone who requested them, so Alberto wrote and asked for some.

"I attended a Christian school and met a marvelous American missionary, and I admired that country," Alberto told friends and supporters attending a TWR event. "I spent a lot of time 'traveling' across America with those maps and dreaming about living there and being an architect."

Those aspirations changed when he attended a youth retreat at the age of 17. "For the first time, I felt the call from God to be a pastor," he said. "That was not my plan but God's plan."

So, in 1963, at the age of 20, Alberto enrolled in the Baptist seminary in Havana. But on Nov. 26, 1965, his life took a dramatically dark turn.

The state of affairs for Christians in Cuba was exceedingly difficult. In fact, during that year more than 50 Baptist pastors were tried and condemned. Alberto's fiery trial came nearly six years after Fidel Castro overthrew Fulgencio Batista's government in an armed revolt. Four years after the botched Bay of Pigs invasion by 1,400 Cuban exiles on the southwestern coast of Cuba. Three years after the world waited, seemingly on the brink of nuclear war, for a peaceful resolution to the Cuban missile crisis, precipitated when Castro began hiding Soviet medium-range ballistic missiles on Cuban soil and the United States responded with a naval quarantine of the island.

All these events occurred after Trans World Radio had begun reaching Cuba with evangelical programs from its new radio station, located roughly 1,000 miles away on the Caribbean island of Bonaire. But Alberto never listened to such radio programs.

Two years after Castro seized power, Alberto said, Christian bookstores and schools were closed, Christian radio programming was prohibited, and the last shipment of Bibles was destroyed at the Havana port. Many Christians fled the country. Some even abandoned their faith. With communism firmly entrenched, many on the island were afraid to go to church and declare their faith because it would cause them great difficulties.

Alberto, nevertheless, remained committed to his faith and God's call to pastoral ministry. Within months of graduating, he was leading four churches to substitute for incarcerated pastors.

Then, one morning in November 1965, he had to report to authorities for what he thought would be mandatory military service. Instead, the 22-year-old would be among a thousand fellow students who would be classified as "social scum" and relegated to an agricultural labor camp for "re-education."

So it was that Alberto, against his will for almost three years, was interned in this Military Units to Aid Production (UMAP) camp that had just been built in the center of the island nation. It would house "dangerous delinquents" considered to be "enemies of the revolution" – including "criminals, tramps, junkies and homosexuals." The camp's primary purpose was "for these young people to change their attitudes, to educate them, to shape them, to redeem them, to prevent them from becoming parasites who are incapable of producing anything, or counter-revolutionary delinquents, or common delinquents, useless beings for society."

"Because of the Marxist-Leninist ideology that the revolution was establishing in Cuba, it was obvious that the government did not want to have any religious people in the armed forces," Alberto wrote in his memoir titled *God Doesn't Come in My Office.*

Alberto González Muñoz (right) is joined by Pastor Alexeide Rubio Dominguez in baptizing a young man in this 2017 photo. Alexeide came to faith in Christ through TWR programming from Bonaire.

"You're here for engaging in unacceptable behavior within our society," an officer barked when the first 120 men arrived. "Today you have entered this unit, but nobody knows if you'll ever get out."

Thousands more would hear that same disdainful message over the coming months. "Because everything depended on you changing your way of thinking, it was never known exactly how many such military units were created, but there were many," Alberto said.

"On Monday, Nov. 29, the routine of our new life began. We awoke at 5 in the morning and were ordered to fall in wearing only our underwear to do exercises, suffering the intense cold of the dawn," Alberto wrote. "We shivered all over until the exercise warmed us. After that was breakfast, and at 7, the infantry classes began."

Then they toiled in the seemingly endless sugar-cane fields for 12 hours – sometimes up to 18 hours. They returned to their barracks exhausted, their muscles on fire.

The grueling physical grind was hard enough for Alberto. But the emotional toll of being separated from his wife-to-be, Miriam, leaving the seminary and the churches he attended, and being taunted for his beliefs, was almost unbearable. In fact, he reached his breaking point, his "crisis of faith."

"Why me, God? I've been faithful to you," he agonized in prayer.

"Please take me, take me. I don't want to wake up tomorrow. I don't want to be in this same place again."

But Alberto did wake up. And he returned to the sugar-cane fields and worked hard along with his Christian friends. However, he'd soon receive soul-stirring hope.

Family members were permitted on occasion to visit. During one get-together, Miriam gave Alberto a small transistor radio. His mother had bought it for him, and Miriam smuggled it into the camp. During the late hours in the fields under the cover of darkness, he and his friends listened to music.

One night, while searching for their music program, they picked up Trans World Radio's broadcast from Bonaire. "It was the first time I had heard such a radio station," Alberto wrote. "Listening to biblical messages and to Christian music amid such circumstances was an unexpected and valuable comfort. The Bible studies filled our hearts and renewed our strength."

Alberto and his friends continued to listen to TWR. "When we worked at night during the harvest, we took turns going deeper into the furrows of cane, hiding and listening for a few minutes," he said. "If there was no work and we went to bed early, I would cover my head with the sheet, and pressing the radio to my ear, listen to the broadcasts. Every night there was a message of faith and hope that helped us to face our difficulties."

LEFT: A family prays together in the kitchen of their home in the city of Bayamo, Cuba. "The Cuban people are hungry for God," says Cuban TWR broadcaster Alberto González Muñoz.
ABOVE: Muñoz in the broadcast studio. "They needed a Cuban voice because they were receiving so many letters from Cuba," he said of his opportunity to begin producing a program from Bonaire in 2009.

God ministered profoundly to Alberto through those broadcasts. He restored him. "It felt like God was with us in that camp," he later told Byron Tyler, host of Bott Radio Network's *Mid-South View Point.* "We were not receiving letters from many people. The Baptist seminary students and I thought that we had been forgotten by everybody. So to listen to that TWR program in the middle of the night, when we were thinking that, it reminded us that God had not forgotten us. He was telling us: 'I am with you. I have a purpose, and I am going to use you.'"

During that interview, Alberto said he had to learn – the hard way – a fundamental transforming lesson on pride. "I was like this proud man, who had been keeping my faith while others were abandoning theirs," he explained. "But I believe that God sent me to that place because I needed to know that only the grace of God is possible to sustain us in those terrible circumstances. I had no strength to do that. I had to recognize that I am nobody without God and without his grace. And only then could I preach the gospel to the people around me."

The UMAP camp closed after three years. Alberto, who had married Miriam during one of his leaves while at camp, returned to seminary and became a full-time pastor and a prominent leader of Cuban Baptists. They have a son, David, and two daughters, Lilly and Leydis, along with seven grandchildren – six boys and one girl. Their adult children are all following Jesus and ministering in Cuba!

Alberto did have an opportunity to live in the United States, not as an architect but as a minister of the gospel. After visiting and preaching at a Spanish-speaking church in Los Angeles, Alberto was asked to take up the pastorate – and to bring his family.

But God didn't give him peace. "In my mind and heart, I felt it was impossible for me to abandon my people back in Cuba," Alberto told the group of TWR friends and supporters. "God called me there, and I believe they needed me. So I turned [the offer in Los Angeles] down and returned to Cuba."

In the late 2000s, the Lord blessed Alberto with an additional pastoral opportunity he never could have envisioned while slaving away in that UMAP camp more than four decades prior. In 2009, TWR asked him to begin producing a program – *Messages of Faith and Hope* – which would be beamed from Bonaire toward Cuba!

"I was really surprised," he said. "They needed a Cuban voice because they were receiving so many letters from Cuba."

At that point, Alberto choked back his emotions. His heart stirs when he remembers when he was in the UMAPs and first heard the programs from the Bonaire station. "It was impossible for me to imagine all those years ago that one day I would be a preacher of the Word of God with the Trans World Radio ministry. This was amazing."

Messages of Faith and Hope examines from a biblical perspective common situations that Cubans face in everyday life. "It's an evangelistic and at the same time a discipleship program, through which we try to reach all Cubans with the purest biblical teaching," he said.

The broadcast generates about 2,000 letters each year from listeners. Alberto was especially touched by responses that arrived from a village tucked away in the Sierra Maestra, a mountain range in southeast Cuba that rises abruptly from the coast. He decided to hold a listener rally there.

Alberto and another pastor, very excited, traveled from Havana to the small town of Playa El Francés, where they hoped to personally meet those who were writing to them. "But when we arrived, to our surprise there was a very large group of brothers and sisters who had converted to Christ by listening to TWR's broadcasts in Spanish," he said. "And they had already organized a very faithful church, which they called Fe y Esperanza [Faith and Hope]."

Alberto has returned repeatedly to that place, accompanied by TWR brothers and sisters, to baptize the new believers constantly joining the congregation. The pastor of the church, Brother Alexeide Rubio, also committed his life to Christ while listening to TWR. "He insists that everything he knows about the Bible and the Christian faith he learned listening to TWR programming from Bonaire," noted Alberto, who retired in 2023 but will continue recording programs for TWR.

That's the power of God!

"The Cuban people are hungry for God," Alberto told Tyler's Bott Radio audience. "This is our moment. This is the time for Cuban preachers and Cuban Christians to reach our people with the saving message of the gospel of Christ."

SECTION III

Waves Around a Turbulent World

THERE'S NO DENYING that our world is full of challenging – and dangerous – places to minister. War, famine and persecution all contribute to the difficulty of reaching people. In fact, the Bible teaches that the Christian life itself is warfare, with the Enemy bent on devouring us and destroying everything for which we labor. Yet TWR has never shied away from advancing the kingdom of God into areas that need the hope of Jesus the most and reaching spiritually thirsty people with living water. Tough places are not impenetrable. In fact, TWR specializes in overcoming the barriers that prevent the gospel from getting to those hard-to-reach places. Media is perfect for such a task. We are committed to taking the gospel to the ends of the earth – whatever it takes, whatever the sacrifice.

The apostle Paul conveyed two critical truths to the churches in Corinth. First, in 2 Corinthians 12:9: "And He has said to me, 'My grace is sufficient for you, for power is perfected in weakness.' Most gladly, therefore, I will rather boast about my weaknesses, so that the power of Christ may dwell in me." Second, in 2 Corinthians 9:8-9: "And God is able to make all grace overflow to you, so that, always having all sufficiency in everything, you may have an abundance for every good deed." TWR missionaries and staff have experienced those passages in real life. No matter where in the world God has called TWR, his grace has been sufficient for every single project, program and person!

"Deliver me from my enemies, O my God;

set me securely on high away from those who

rise up against me. Deliver me from those who

do iniquity and save me from men of bloodshed."

– PSALM 59:1-2

9

A Voice for the Gospel in Times of War

ROSTISLAV BABENKO FELT the sudden nudge: Call your friend.

As deputy director of TWR Ukraine, Babenko was busy enough already. It was March 2022, and his country had been at war with Russia for less than a month. From Ukraine's perspective, it had not gone well, and Babenko found himself thrust into added responsibilities. Primarily, he was helping his fellow Ukrainians evacuate areas that were under attack. His life was constantly in danger.

But when the Holy Spirit brought his friend to mind, Babenko called him even though they hadn't seen each other for two years.

His friend was in Kharkiv, Ukraine's second-largest city, and clearly was distraught. The friend said he just wanted himself and his family to die and "be over with it."

Babenko didn't hesitate. Immediately, he made the perilous drive to

Kharkiv to get his friend and his family out of danger. During the drive, his friend mentioned that he had grown distant from God during the previous two years. But in the midst of the violence and chaos, he recognized God's presence in the fact that Babenko was there to rescue him and his family.

TWR UKRAINE, OUR national partner in that country, observed its 30th anniversary in 2022 under trying circumstances. Director Alexander Chmut and his family temporarily took refuge in a children's home, and the military assigned Chmut to dig trenches. Most staff members remained in the country, but some family members were evacuated elsewhere. After Chmut and the staff returned to the capital city of Kyiv, broadcasts and daily life were interrupted by missile strikes and power outages. Programs were sometimes broadcast by candlelight and sometimes from the basement of Chmut's home.

TWR's mission is to reach the world for Christ by mass media so that lasting fruit is produced. Since we do, in fact, reach most of the world, we are affected by most of the world's calamities. In such times, God's purposes are still accomplished.

TWR leadership understands that it's often when crisis situations occur that people are the most open to the gospel. Political situations often change dramatically, but the kingdom of God never changes, and it is the only true source of hope.

RUSSIA AND UKRAINE have a common heritage that goes back more than a thousand years, notes Maria Wedel, TWR's coordinator for Russia, Ukraine and Belarus.

Kyiv, the capital of modern Ukraine, was at the center of the first Slavic state, Kievan Rus, Wedel said. Both Ukraine and Russia emerged from this historical part of the country, which is also known as Old Russia. Vladimir I, prince of Novgorod and grand prince of Kyiv, adopted the Christian Orthodox faith and was baptized in A.D. 988.

Ihor Yaremchuk, rector of Irpin Biblical Seminary in Ukraine, speaks from the war-ravaged ruins of the seminary. During the first year of the war, the seminary was shelled, taken over by the Russian military and then reclaimed by Ukraine. Yaremchuk is producer of a TWR Ukraine program called *Biblical Statement*.

Russian President Vladimir Putin describes this as the moment when the Russian and Ukrainian people became one, Wedel said. "However, this did not save Ukraine from being repeatedly divided and fragmented by competing powers over the past 10 centuries."

Russia, Ukraine and Belarus were all part of the Soviet Union. During much of the Soviet era, Trans World Radio was a voice of the gospel in the wilderness. Though not welcomed by the government, the message had a way of getting through.

NICK SIEMENS, WHO retired from TWR in 2019 after 42 years of service in Europe, said he was a listener long before he was a staff member.

"We boys found out that if you put an antenna between the house and some kind of tree in the direction of the radio station, then it may increase the reception," recalled Siemens, who grew up in Latvia when it was part of the Soviet Union.

Siemens said his grandmother was the "greatest living testimony" bringing him to faith in Christ, but what he heard on the radio via TWR was a contributing factor. He asked Jesus into his heart at age 13, he said, and at 15 was baptized – late at night, in secret.

Russian and Ukrainian were among the first 23 languages spoken on what became TWR when it was still The Voice of Tangier airing out of Morocco in North Africa. A program guide from 1956 shows 15-minute programs being aired in both languages. After TWR was shut out of Tangier, the languages and programs were broadcast out of Monte Carlo.

Early programs were produced by Ukrainian immigrants in North America via the Ukrainian Baptist Union of Canada and of the United States, Siemens said. The broadcasts were by shortwave, which was widely available across the Soviet Union at that time.

"Voice of America broadcast at that time in Russian, so did Germany, so did Radio France Internationale, Sweden, Korea, Japan – all of them had Russian-language programs aired on shortwave toward the Soviet Union," Siemens explained. "I would almost say 90% to 95% of the Soviet households did have shortwave receivers."

THE IMPACT OF TWR behind the Iron Curtain started to become known after the fall of the Soviet Union at the end of 1991, Siemens said. "What was said by many pastors after the Soviet Union collapsed was that a good deal of the people who came to the church and accepted the Lord and expressed a desire to be baptized had their first encounter with Christianity by radio," he noted.

As a program producer who was also able to translate across several languages, Siemens often found himself in contact with his counterparts who had served for the Soviet government. Among them were specialists who had built the antennas intended to jam TWR's content. But in the post-Soviet era, those same specialists responded to the mention of TWR from Monte Carlo with warm greetings.

"Now it was a door opener," Siemens said.

Over time, more and more of the program production was transferred to the countries where the programs would be heard. That led to the establishment of TWR Ukraine as a national partner in 1992.

IN UKRAINE TODAY, Chmut leads a youthful team who produce a robust array of programming, both in radio and in social media. The disruption and danger from the war only seemed to inspire them to increase their efforts.

Video has proven to be an especially effective means of communicating hope and truth during the war.

One video, shot as Chmut was walking to a worksite to dig trenches during the early phases of the war, had attracted 7.5 million views by early 2024.

The team produced programs that reflected the troubled lives of a nation at war – Ukrainians ministering to Ukrainians as they shared in suffering. This included a series of full-length video documentaries featuring TWR Ukraine's Andriy Gotsulyak. The series title is literally translated as *How Are You There?* It might be understood as *How Are You Coping?* as each program focuses on believers in a particular Ukrainian city and how the war has changed their lives.

The TWR Ukraine team also boldly entered new social media territory, determined to reach Ukrainians where they are. These include the short video clips on Instagram known as reels and videos on the TikTok app. A 2022 TikTok featuring Chmut attracted 296,000 views.

"We receive many testimonies of how people's lives are changed after listening to our programs and watching our videos," Chmut wrote in September 2022. "Never before in the history of TWR Ukraine have we received as many responses to our programs as we're receiving during the war."

This has been true in Belarus and Russia as well as Ukraine, Wedel said. "The war has opened people more to the gospel."

·|||·

THE DIVISIONS BETWEEN countries don't extend to the believers in those countries, Wedel said.

"The teams in [Belarus, Russia and Ukraine] have already worked together in some ways, and even now they are not at odds," she said.

The larger TWR world responded to a region in crisis. In the first months of the war, TWR lost a significant AM frequency for the region. TWR soon responded by adding a second AM frequency for the region and used its Guam station to broadcast via shortwave.

We also turned to our CAT West transmitter, operating from an undisclosed location in Central Asia, to increase coverage to both sides of the conflict.

"It's a steerable signal," Libby explained. "It is also one of the primary ways that we're able to reach on the air into Ukraine and western Russia."

TWR also created a 24/7 livestream called Voice of Ukraine Hope Radio, available to anyone with internet access.

For refugees from the war, TWR partnered with Operation Mobilization (OM) to supply a thousand pocket-size power banks. The devices, which include links to the two organizations, allow refugees to recharge cellphones and other gadgets when no power outlets are available.

To help meet the special expenses associated with the war, TWR set up a Ukraine-Russia Crisis Fund. The money has been used for everything from helping the family of a TWR Ukraine technician who were left with no belongings after missile attacks to sustaining broadcasts under new and difficult circumstances. The war had destructive impacts on Belarus and Russia as well as Ukraine, which is why the crisis fund was available for special needs throughout the region.

The generosity of TWR donors has been so meaningful. But prayer is the most strategic tool, Siemens said.

"I would ask people to pray," he said. "Pray for the ... political leaders, pray for TWR local leaders. ... Pray for those who listen. Pray for those who may get to listen for the first time; for the content providers, for God to give them wisdom to feed the people the kind of spiritual food people need today.

"And especially pray for the antennas and for the transmitter sites, that God would keep them going, keep them strong."

Early in the war, TWR Ukraine staff members had to say goodbye to some of their wives and children, who took refuge in other countries. Here, Alexander Chmut bids farewell to a family member, whose face was obscured for security purposes.

A man surveys one of the many Ukrainian buildings damaged by shelling during the war. Since the invasion of Ukraine began on Feb. 24, 2022, many things have changed, but the need for Jesus is as great as ever.

"My foes have trampled upon me all day long,

for they are many who fight proudly against me.

When I am afraid, I will put my trust in You.

In God, whose word I praise,

in God I have put my trust;

I shall not be afraid.

What can mere man do to me?

— PSALM 56:2-4

10

A Special Heart and Burden for Nigeria

THERE'S NO DENYING that rampant religious extremism and brutal ethnic violence are bedeviling Nigeria. This lethal reign of terror has devastated Africa's largest nation, which is also one of the world's most populated countries.

According to Open Doors, research for its 2022 World Watch List revealed that in 2021, "more Christians were murdered for their faith in Nigeria than in any other country, with more than 4,650 believers killed." That accounted for nearly 80% of Christian deaths worldwide, making "Nigeria the world's most violent place for Christians – for the second consecutive year." When Open Doors issued its 2023 World Watch List, the death toll was just as dire. "Of the 5,621 Christians killed for their faith in 2022, 90% of these were from Nigeria alone."

Toward the end of 2023, another religious freedom watchdog group – International Christian Concern (ICC) – issued a frightening warning about Nigeria. "It is arguably the most dangerous place to be a Christian in the world today." The report went on to say, "Whether the world acknowledges the plight of Nigerian Christians or not, the country has become a burial ground for Christians."

And once again, Open Doors declared in its 2024 World Watch List that "more believers are killed for their faith in Nigeria each year than everywhere else in the world, combined. The attacks are often brutal in nature and can involve destruction of properties, abductions for ransom, sexual violence and death. Believers are stripped of their livelihoods and driven from their homes, leaving a trail of grief and trauma."

Believers in Jesus Christ keep getting murdered. Churches are being bombed. And several million people have been displaced within the country.

This seemingly unending mayhem and death appears hopeless to reverse. As long as militants continue to terrorize the country's northern states and as long as Fulani herders, who are primarily Muslims looking for land where their cattle, goats and sheep can graze, clash with non-Fulani Christian farmers, Nigeria will be beset by perpetual violence and strife.

TWR has not flinched in the face of this insurgency. In fact, it has heeded the clarion calls to expand its program lineup being beamed toward Nigeria. Its highly talented and committed staff have bolstered the number of evangelistic programs so that more non-Christian listeners can hear messages of love, redemption and reconciliation. TWR has also increased the number of biblically sound broadcasts geared toward believers, helping them to grow, stand firm and proclaim the gospel with fearlessness. And despite the dangers, Nigerian brothers in Christ are displaying a courageous witness as they crisscross their beleaguered nation, even to the North, to distribute radios and other helpful materials and to arrange meetings and gatherings.

The team in West Africa has also invested sizably in hardware and equipment, replacing a once giant voice in the region. For nearly 60 years, the missionary organization SIM transmitted programs across the region from its powerful radio station ELWA (Eternal Love Winning Africa) in Liberia. It was the first missionary radio station in all of Africa. But multiple civil wars caused pervasive damage to the compound, and its signal tragically went quiet.

That's when TWR was able to step in and fill the void. TWR's Africa director Stephen Boakye-Yiadom, who was from Ghana, had a vision for West Africa because its people, too, needed Jesus. For years, TWR searched for a suitable location within the region from which to broadcast, but none of those initial sites panned out. Eventually, in his perfect providence, God opened a unique door, and on Feb. 1, 2008, TWR began broadcasting the good news of Jesus in multiple languages from what's known as the West Africa Transmitting Station, or WATS.

What's amazing is that these programs, which unequivocally herald the God of the Bible as the one true God and Jesus Christ as the Lord who was crucified and resurrected and is coming again, originate from a land steeped in Voodoo.

"From WATS, we were covering nine countries, but over the years, it became more and more apparent that we needed something more focused for Nigeria," explained Garth Kennedy, a veteran TWR missionary who serves as the Africa director for broadcast station operations. "The cry of the people was for more programming. But since airtime on the first transmitter was fully booked, we couldn't add anything to that."

TWR President Libby cited a survey from the BBC that found there was a vast listening audience within Nigeria for medium wave. "I remember speaking to a leader in another organization whom I knew fairly well in Nigeria, and he encouraged us when he said, 'If you're going to influence the northern part of the country, you're not going to do it through politics or with the military,

A Nigerian couple hears the Word of God through radio. "Only God could have arranged the astonishing circumstances for us to broadcast to this region," said Garth Kennedy, Africa director for broadcast station operations.

but the only way you can influence it is through Jesus and the hope that the kingdom of God can bring to the people day after day, night after night.'"

What was the answer? "We added a second transmitter directed toward Nigeria," Kennedy said. "And yeah, only God could have arranged the astonishing circumstances for us to broadcast to this region from the site on which WATS is now located. We learned to lean more on him, for sure."

This project was bathed in prayer. Ground was broken in August 2018. The Lord provided the transmitter from Switzerland and, just as the Lord did for the Bonaire and other transmitter projects, he raised up donors sprinkled around the world who gave sacrificially to underwrite the project. Locally employed and trained technicians installed the mammoth tower. "They did a really good job, working through the dry season, which is the hot season as well," Kennedy said. "When the guys came off the tower, we applauded them. We celebrated that milestone. It was really good for the team."

Also helping to support the work of TWR Africa – and to provide for the education of the local staff – the WATS crew has planted thousands of trees across the sprawling property. They believe that God gave them the land, and they strive to practice good stewardship of it – and to demonstrate the gospel to each other and to those in need throughout their surrounding communities. Teak, cashew, moringa, mango and mahogany trees dot the landscape. And they plant and harvest maize, as well as manage two dozen beehives. God has blessed!

Finally, exactly 12 years to the day after programs began airing on the original 100,000-watt transmitter, TWR expanded the reach of WATS by adding a 150,000-watt AM transmitter, known as Oasis, to reach into Nigeria.

"The concept of 'oasis' is prevalent in the Bible, where people would come to an oasis and rest, be refreshed and take the water," explained Branko Bjelajac, international vice president for TWR in Africa. "It was appropriately named."

Kennedy added, "What excites us is that we are able to continually declare God's good news into a conflict-prone region and to people who are suffering and into areas where Christians are being chased out or killed. This keeps us going!"

Not only has adding the Oasis transmitter helped meet the huge gospel-broadcasting needs of Nigeria and the surrounding countries of Niger, Cameroon and Benin, but the original AM transmitter also has been freed up to provide more hours of programming in the many other heart languages of West Africa.

Listener reports indicate that transmissions are reaching into the northeastern region, considered the base of terrorism in the country. This is particularly true in Maiduguri, the capital city of Borno state and principal trading hub for that area. "Before we launched, testing to Maiduguri proved that our signal was excellent," Bjelajac said. "That's still the case."

God is truly moving, and hearts are being touched. A refugee camp for internally displaced people is in Maiduguri. One listener told TWR: "Many people here in the camp are traumatized due to the experiences that brought them here. The messages from TWR are changing our lives. Listening to the messages is bringing healing to those going through trauma."

Another listener brought uplifting news: "I know two people in Maiduguri who were from Muslim backgrounds, but through these programs and the Bibles TWR shared with us, they started reading the Bible, and today they have given their lives to Jesus and have become Christians."

The home of the West Africa Transmitting Station is seen in this 2017 photo. After searching for years to find a suitable location, TWR began broadcasting from this site on Feb. 1, 2008.

One missions agency leader there said: "I have received information from one of the core states in the north where people are listening to the radio programs of TWR and where distributions have been made. The Lord has brought a soul to himself, and we have been called upon and the new convert will be brought to us for discipleship. I just want to encourage the hearts of the brethren who are laboring with us in TWR and make you understand that our labor is not in vain."

These results bring great joy to Abdoulaye Sangho, TWR's international director for West and Central Africa. He knows personally the impact that Christians can make in the lives of Muslims in West Africa. From an Islamic background in Mali and having lost his parents and grandparents by the time he was 10 years old, Sangho gave his life to Christ through the influence of Christian missionaries who reached out to him in love when he was struggling.

Now serving with TWR, he has a grand vision for the continent: "I have a dream that every African will hear and understand the Word of God in his own language, and that one day, the African church will grow, not only in number but in depth, to become a church of mission, reaching all Africa and beyond."

"From the end of the earth I call to
You when my heart is faint;
lead me to the rock that is higher than I.
For You have been a refuge for me,
a tower of strength against the enemy.
Let me dwell in Your tent forever;
let me take refuge in the shelter of Your wings."

— PSALM 61:2-4

11

The Secret Towers

IN A FLORIDA meeting room far, far from home, Abraham* heard a familiar voice.

Abraham quickly pulled out his phone, tapped it a few times and put it to his ear. A broad grin swept across his face, and he hurried over to the man in the room who had that same voice.

"You're him!" Abraham said. "You're him! You're the voice I've been listening to for the past 20 years!"

Abraham is from Kabul, the capital city of Afghanistan. Twenty years earlier, he had left Islam to follow Jesus. As a new believer, he turned to the radio for discipleship. He listened to programs from Pamir Productions, TWR's partner in Afghanistan. He recorded them, memorized them and lived by them. He attended an underground church and continued listening to the programs. They had a cascading effect on others around him.

One of the voices he often heard came from a man named Achmed.*

Now, Abraham was with a group of Afghan believers who had escaped to the U.S. during the Taliban takeover in 2021. It was at an annual gathering of people concerned for Afghanistan in June-July 2022. Mike Ball, a TWR strategist who attended the conference, heard the story from a Pamir Productions staffer who was in the room at the time.

It was a power-packed, joyful event, Ball said, the first time many Afghan Christians from throughout North America had been together in one place since the fall of Kabul.

Abraham said the radio programs had helped him grow strong in God's Word. Achmed said that for years while writing and recording the programs, he had wondered if anyone was listening.

Now they were face-to-face: the mentor and the disciple he had never met.

Reaching people like Abraham in places such as Afghanistan and beyond was always a driving force for Werner Kroemer, who retired in 2016 after 22 years of full-time ministry with TWR.

A man pauses to listen to a broadcast at a marketplace in the Central Asian nation of Kyrgyzstan. TWR is able to reach Central Asia through the 500,000-watt PANI transmitter in an undisclosed location.

"According to my understanding, TWR's calling was and still is broadcasting to closed countries," Kroemer said during an interview at the TWR office in Bratislava, Slovakia.

How does a ministry open doors to a closed country?

"You have to do it primarily from outside the country," said Lauren Libby, president of TWR. "And going outside the country means that you either use digital or broadcast means, and we do both."

The spiritual needs of people from the Middle East, across the Persian-speaking world, and on into Central and South Asia led to the establishment of several transmitters – known as CAT West, PANI and Silk Road – whose locations are so sensitive that TWR doesn't disclose them publicly. Here's a look at each.

THE CAT IN CAT West stands for Central Asia Transmitter. It started in 1996 with TWR purchasing airtime on a million-watt AM transmitter, Kroemer said, to reach Central Asia, the Persian-speaking world and the Middle East. To put that in context, the most powerful AM transmitters allowed in the United States are 50,000 watts.

Then, with "lots of prayer and by a number of miracles of the Lord," TWR in 2003-06 developed a second million-watt AM transmitting facility to more effectively cover Central Asia and the Persian-speaking world, Kroemer said.

At the same time, the Lord granted favor to Felix Widmer, who was responsible for TWR's ministry in that area, with the development of programs meeting an urgent need of the underground church. He orchestrated the partnership of major mission organizations in developing the *Discipleship on the Air* program series.

The site recently has been updated, Libby said. "We've just worked on replacing the old transmitter with a solid-state transmitter which is far more efficient."

The new transmitter is about 94% efficient, Libby said, compared to the original, which was about 30% efficient. That means much less energy will be needed to power the transmitter.

The money for the new transmitter was raised in about six months, he said. That was largely on the strength of a TWR supporter who asked Libby if the ministry had any particular needs. Libby told him about the need for the new transmitter at the CAT West site. A day later, the individual called and said, "We'd like to pick up $900,000 of that."

"This is a primary voice into the Middle East along with our digital voice," Libby said, reaching places such as Iran and Saudi Arabia.

And people in hard-to-reach places are hearing the Word.

"Every night my church is your radio program," a listener to those Farsi broadcasts wrote. "My fellowship is with your radio program. Sometimes I am unable to meet with other believers for two to three weeks. Thank you for helping me grow in my faith and to get to know my Savior more and more."

PANI STANDS FOR Pakistan, Afghanistan and North India. It refers to the region reached, which is predominantly Muslim.

TWR's ministry director for Central Asia at the time, Willi Epp, was able to build a relationship with the owners of what was then called CAT East, which broadcast on AM, also known as medium wave. TWR started to broadcast from there in 2003, Kroemer said. "It gave us a unique possibility to broadcast into the eastern part of Central Asia and also to the Uyghur [people] in China."

"This relationship was very helpful when we started to work on the possibility to broadcast to Pakistan and Afghanistan in 2007, but it took years until the Lord opened the door for TWR," Kroemer said. "TWR had no way, really, to reach those countries on medium wave, so we prayed."

What followed was a succession of contracts signed and annulled, directors of the CAT East company being hired and fired, transmitter deliveries

rejected, and round after round of "endless negotiations," Kroemer said. "Every new director wanted to have his own contract. It went on and on."

The $1.5 million for the PANI transmitter was raised in about eight months, which was an amazing act of God.

Broadcasts in the Dari and Pashto languages began with full power on March 24, 2014. By the end of 2014, broadcasts were reaching Pakistan, Afghanistan and North India in 10 languages.

The sacrificial giving of many individuals to both transmitter projects is a testimony to how the Spirit of God begins to move, Libby said. "We've found that as we move forward in vision, God responds by motivating people's hearts to be involved in it."

The 500,000-watt PANI transmitter is a tremendous tool, Libby said. People in the region also can follow TWR digitally, he said, "but they have to be very careful because securitywise if you check in on your cellphone or you check in on the internet, that's a traceable event. Listening on the air is not a traceable event."

The $1.5 million needed for the transmitter was raised in eight months. Broadcasts in the Dari and Pashto languages began with full power on March 24, 2014, and the number of languages quickly grew from there. The PANI transmitter reaches listeners in Pakistan, Afghanistan and North India.

That's particularly true in Afghanistan, he said, and even more so for women in Afghanistan.

In one of the world's most highly restricted countries, the gospel is being proclaimed through radio.

"My daughter started listening to *Sadaye Zindagi [Sound of Life]* and introduced us to it," a listener to the Dari language programs in Afghanistan wrote. "Now we all listen and love your radio programs, especially the Bible stories."

THE CAT EAST transmitter that had been used to bring gospel messages to Central Asia since 2003 reached the end of its life in autumn 2016 with no replacement parts available. That created the need for what became the Silk Road transmitter.

Negotiations to replace CAT East started as early as 2013, but no breakthrough had been reached. Although some broadcasting continued by other means, it had to be scaled back substantially.

The 200,000-watt Silk Road transmitter, which first began broadcasting on June 10, 2019, has a potential listening audience of 60 million, primarily in Kazakhstan, Uzbekistan, Turkmenistan, Kyrgyzstan and Tajikistan. As of early 2024, 31 AM programs were being broadcast in a total of five languages.

As with PANI, the Silk Road negotiations were complex. At the beginning of 2018, once again a new general director was appointed who invited Kroemer to give the idea of this transmitter project another try. Although retired, Kroemer traveled with Willi Epp and Daryl Renshaw, a TWR vice president, for talks between TWR and the company owner in May 2018, he said. Differences in wording eventually were worked out, and the contracts were signed late on a Tuesday, after which Renshaw and Kroemer returned home.

"On Thursday morning, the first thing when we opened our computer, we were told that the general director [of the company] and his executive staff were fired," Kroemer recalled. "But then his successor came, and I knew this gentleman from earlier." After fresh talks, the successor agreed to honor the contract.

KROEMER SAID THESE transmitters fulfilled God's plan, not man's. "It was not our master plan, as people always seem to say," he noted. "This is a huge misunderstanding. We were praying and asking the Lord for guidance. ... And we trusted the Lord to lead and guide us, and he did."

Each of the transmitter agreements required years of hard work as well as fervent prayer. Opportunities had to be explored, funds had to be raised, technical ability had to be put to use. Engineers, especially Helmut Menzel and Ruedi Baertschi, played an essential role, Kroemer said. As much as anything, negotiating skills were needed. Reaching an agreement required a relationship between the parties, built over time.

"They are not doing business with you if they don't trust you," Kroemer said.

Through all those transmitters, the gospel now is being proclaimed by AM radio in places that are difficult for traditional missionaries to reach.

AM was and remains common in most of the countries reached through these transmitters, Kroemer said. Often, people listen to a national broadcasting company on AM.

"People had these cheap medium-wave radios at home," he said. "People can afford it. And the positive thing for radio is, number one, with radio you cannot identify who is listening."

They listen, and lives are transformed. In Uzbekistan, one of the countries reached by the Silk Road transmitter, a listener wrote: "My cousin who works in a sewing shop recently accepted Christ. She told her friend the gospel, and they listened to the radio together. After some time, her friend said that she also wanted to accept Christ."

During the development of the CAT West transmitters, Tom Lowell (until 2003) and David Tucker (2003-2007) were presidents and CEOs of TWR. The PANI and the Silk Road transmitters were developed with

Lauren Libby as president. Kroemer was the point man for all these projects, first as European regional director, later as global vice president.

That certainly speaks to Kroemer's experience in the region, his patience and his skill as a negotiator. But negotiating skills aren't the most important thing, Kroemer said.

"We are in spiritual warfare, and for spiritual warfare you need spiritual weapons," he said. "The only weapon which we have is prayer.

"So if we don't pray, nothing will happen."

"The Lord also will be a stronghold for the oppressed, a stronghold in times of trouble; and those who know Your name will put their trust in You. For You, O Lord, have not forsaken those who seek You."

— PSALM 9:9-10

12

God's Love and Care Are Evident in Central Asia

G OD IS UNQUESTIONABLY answering prayer as TWR friends are asking God to soften hearts and draw men, women, boys and girls to himself throughout Central Asia and Pakistan, Afghanistan and North India.

This region was certainly rocked in 2021 when a major insurgent offensive led to the fall of the Kabul-based Islamic Republic of Afghanistan and the capture of its capital city by the Taliban. Two years later, the country was still facing a state of crisis – with a stricken economy, the threat of famine and two-thirds of Afghans reportedly needing humanitarian aid.

But regardless, rejoice with us as God brings people to his Son, the Lord Jesus Christ, not only in Afghanistan but also elsewhere throughout the troubled region. The Lord is forgiving their sin and restoring them to the right relationship with him that he created them to have. New believers are growing in Christ, becoming like him and serving him with boldness.

ZAFAR* LIVES IN northern Tajikistan. He received radio sets from TWR with recorded Christian programs and has distributed them to his home group and to other families. "We are all very grateful that we can listen to these programs. We use them to grow together in our faith."

BILAL* HAILED A taxi in Kyrgyzstan and ended up sharing it with two women. During their journey, the taxi driver turned on the radio. Bilal, a young Christian, was surprised. He recognized the broadcast from TWR, one that he faithfully listens to! The two women began discussing what they were hearing. Overhearing their conversation, Bilal happily told the women that he personally knows the producers of this program. In fact, right there in the taxi, he called one of the producers and told him how much the two women liked the broadcast and that they wanted to know more about God. Then he invited the two women to visit one of the Christian communities in the region.

NIGORA* AND HER husband in Uzbekistan listen to TWR's programs every day. Her husband is blind, and the radio is constantly on in their household.

The couple does not keep the teaching to themselves. They're telling their neighbors.

"They're now interested and are faithful listeners," Nigora told TWR. "We are all together with our neighbors and have become your fans.

"Thank you for suitable programs for everyone, for children, for adults and the whole family," she added. "We have only one request: Make your programs longer."

DURING THE COVID-19 pandemic, one woman in a Central Asian country started asking her family pointed questions about the Christian faith.

Her younger sister, who had received a radio and an SD card with TWR programs on it, answered her questions.

"How do you know all the answers to my questions? Don't tell me you're a believer in Christ."

"I have a radio, and together with my family I listen to the Christian programs," the woman's sister replied. "That is how I have learned so many things about Isa al-Masih [Muslims' name for Jesus]. Now I believe in him and continue to listen to the broadcasts. Please pray for my family, that they will also turn to God."

ONE CHRISTIAN LEADER in Central Asia shared this amazing story: "At the time of the Soviet Union, Christians were oppressed and persecuted. Young believers in the army experienced a lot of pressure. When I served in the army in the 1970s, I had an amazing experience. One night, I was woken up and was called into the 'Lenin room,' where the solders usually gathered. A group of soldiers, who had no affiliation to a church, had gathered there secretly to listen to the TWR broadcasts."

Two Afghani teenagers pose for the camera in 2006, during a time when Afghanistan was governed as a constitutional democracy. The resumption of Taliban control in 2021 led to new restrictions for women and girls.

A LISTENER TO PANI broadcasts told TWR: "The situation in our town is very complex. Many people consider themselves Muslims, such as my husband. I used to say to my friends that we are born as Muslims and will die as Muslims. We could not change our faith. But then I started listening to your programs, and I understood what it really means to believe. I came to know Christ through the radio. I cannot read the Bible at home because my husband would kill me or be violent. However, I have an SD card with the Bible programs on it, so I can listen to them secretly. I really like them."

AFSOON* WAS DEEPLY concerned about her neighbor Hamkiya,* who was extremely sick. Afsoon had shared previously about Jesus with her friend, but Hamkiya wasn't interested. Afsoon kept praying for her and asked God for another opportunity to talk with her ailing friend about spiritual matters. One day, Hamkiya opened up about God and asked Afsoon why there are sorrows and evil on this earth if God loves all people. Afsoon shared with her friend what she had been learning from the TWR broadcasts.

"God loves people and cares for them," Afsoon said. "He is not indifferent to pain. He sent his Son to rescue mankind."

At that moment, another neighbor came to visit and showed interest in what they were talking about.

"God is reaching the people," Afsoon told TWR. "Praise be to him!"

ONE LISTENER IS deeply worried about his country. He told TWR: "We do not have peace. ISIS and the Taliban have a lot of control on people. No one can defend themselves. People with power and guns can take anything they want from you. Years ago the borders were open, and you could go to Pakistan or Iran to escape danger, but now the borders are closed, and people have to do what the gunmen require. Please keep Afghanistan in your prayers."

* Not their real names to protect their privacy

"Blessed be the Lord, for He has made marvelous

His lovingkindness to me in a besieged city."

— PSALM 31:21

13

Economic Calamity Can't Halt Ministry

T HE CHRIST FOLLOWERS meet at night, after the day's work has been done.

Three men and three women, one holding a toddler, sing together. One lifts his hands in praise, his shadow crossing the wall of the small living area. Returning to their seats, they share thanksgivings and petitions, then bow together in prayer.

The leader then places a small black cylinder on the coffee table and turns a switch. From that device, the teaching time for the night begins. A voice in their Sinhala language speaks truth from the Word of God. Afterward, the group members discuss the teachings, sing another song and break for the night so they can rest up for the day's labors ahead.

Known as a radio home group, it is one of almost a thousand such groups set up in the South Asia nation of Sri Lanka within the past three years. According to Vinsanda,* TWR Lanka's audio relations supervisor, these are not designed to be local churches but safe places to help people get into the Bible, to grow in their relationship with Jesus Christ and to speak to someone else about their faith.

Vinsanda, whose responsibilities include serving the groups, was a guest on this particular evening, along with his colleague Mewan,* social media coordinator for TWR Lanka, TWR's national partner on the island off the southern tip of India. Also present were Alex Lemus and Clay Perry of the Cary, North Carolina-based TWR Global Marketing and Communications video team.

Perry and Lemus were documenting Sri Lanka's radio home groups in January 2023 on behalf of TWR Canada, which was celebrating its 50th anniversary that same year.

The groups, typically consisting of five to eight people, provide opportunities for spiritual growth built around sound biblical teaching from a media player. These have especially been vital as this troubled nation has had to navigate its latest crisis.

SRI LANKA IS no stranger to violent upheaval and hostility. After gaining independence from British rule in 1948, a 26-year civil war between the mostly Buddhist Sinhalese majority and the mostly Hindu ethnic Tamil minority ripped apart this tropical island from the 1980s till it ended in 2009.

Though a relative calm secured a toehold for the next decade, simmering sectarian and religious tensions still festered. Those flared Easter Sunday in 2019, when coordinated suicide bombing attacks on churches and luxury hotels killed more than 250 people.

These bombings shattered a once robust tourism industry. This was further exacerbated by the COVID-19 pandemic as borders around the world closed and international travel ground to a halt. In 2022, there was a crippling economic downturn, along with soaring inflation and skyrocketing costs for basic goods. Conditions grew even more dire as the war in Ukraine sparked a widespread fuel and food crisis. Discontent turned to anger, which boiled over. People took to the streets to protest, and demonstrators clashed with government troops, despite curfews. Some politicians stepped down.

Despite this economic and political tsunami, TWR's team in Sri Lanka remained faithful to their calling. They continued to speak hope to the nation's 22 million people.

Christians are not immune to difficulties or challenges. The Sri Lankan staff know that. They labor on, clinging to such promises as 1 Corinthians 15:58 – "Therefore, my beloved brothers and sisters, be firm, immovable, always excelling in the work of the Lord, knowing that your labor is not in vain in the Lord" (NASB).

God's protection was evident. "Our co-workers in Sri Lanka have experienced the same hardships as their fellow countrymen," said Jonathan Lee, TWR Asia marketing and communications director. "We thank God for keeping them safe and enabling them to faithfully continue ministering as best they can in the face of such challenges – especially through the limitations of power outages and curfews."

TWR videographers Clay Perry (left) and Alex Lemus film during a 2023 visit to a "radio home group" in Sri Lanka. The groups are designed to be safe places where people can get into the Bible, grow in their relationship with Jesus and speak to others about their faith.

PHOTO BY JONATHAN MITCHELL FOR TWR

TWR's impact has been felt across Sri Lanka. It works with local partners who produce programs in languages spoken by most Sri Lankans: Sinhala and Tamil.

In early 2023, TWR's Lemus and Perry traveled around the southern half of the island, which is about the same size as the U.S. state of West Virginia. The focus is on the south because that is where Sinhala is primarily spoken, they explained. The secondary language of Sri Lanka is Tamil, but more Christian resources are available in that language.

The radio home groups function like small groups in U.S. and other Western churches, except the Bible study is done through listening to the programs. Listeners then discuss what they have learned and pray and fellowship with one another.

"People are coming to Jesus all across Sri Lanka, and these groups are perfect for brand-new believers to get to know him and develop their

A "radio home group" gathers in Sri Lanka to worship and hear teaching on a listening device provided by TWR Lanka.

PHOTO BY JONATHAN MITCHELL FOR TWR

walk with the Lord," said TWR President Lauren Libby. "They're proving instrumental in helping people to study God's Word and to grow in their Christian faith. Lasting fruit is certainly the long-term goal."

TWR Lanka develops its own programs for the groups, so its staff includes two experts in Christian theology to make sure the teaching is sound, Lemus said. They also rely on native Sri Lankan Bible teachers.

Some pastors attend radio home groups to glean additional biblical truth that they can then share with their congregations, Perry said.

Another strategic purpose of the groups is to train believers to bring others to Christ, Perry said. He told the story of a man named Kosala,* who first fully understood the gospel at a radio home group. Kosala then shared the hope of Jesus with a childhood friend, and he prayed for healing when his friend became seriously ill. When the friend recovered, he was much more receptive. So Kosala again presented the claims of Christ, and his friend came to faith. Then his friend shared the gospel with a family that also accepted Christ.

"You just see this multiplication happening, and that's just one story," Perry said.

The radio home groups are set up mostly in rural areas where resources are the most limited, Lemus said. "A lot of people in rural areas don't necessarily have the chance or the resources to go into the city and spend money on a Bible institute or at a Bible course," he added.

Lemus and Perry met others whose lives had been transformed through radio home groups. One was a former Hindu priest who came to know the Lord. Another, the daughter of an aboriginal chief, leads a radio home group.

TWR Lanka's Vinsanda said he envisions anywhere from 6,000 to 10,000 radio home groups eventually will be established in Sri Lanka's rural area.

God's Holy Spirit is unequivocally working throughout the country. One listener told TWR: "I come from a different faith, but through your programs, I accepted Jesus as my Savior. I don't miss any of the programs because they are the only hope for me."

One timely Sinhala program that is reaching Sri Lankans is titled *God's Unique Book*. It examines who God is and what makes him unique. This program geared toward oral learners then moves through Scripture from creation to the cross.

Kasun* is one of its faithful listeners. One day he was tuning the radio to listen to music when he came across *God's Unique Book*. He's paralyzed, having fallen from a tree 20 years ago. He had heard about Jesus but hadn't placed his faith in him. But the more he listened to the program, a spark was lit. "Doctors gave up on me," Kasun said. "After listening to your program, I madly trust in this Jesus. He will heal me. Could you pay a visit to my home and pray for me?"

Someone else wrote: "I follow a different religion but listen regularly to your program. I have a radio and a separate place in my room to listen to it. I highly appreciate the way the speaker teaches. I really love the program. Today's topic really touched my heart. I am seeking after truth."

Another person said he is emboldened by the broadcasts. He said: "Before I became a believer, I had tried just about everything I could think of to help resolve my problems. I worked in Dubai for a bit, but I was struggling financially. So I came back to Sri Lanka and opened a textile shop. Around the same time, I came to learn about Christ and accepted him into my life. My fellow villagers began persecuting me for my faith, which has remained the case till this day. Your program last Saturday motivated me. I am blessed that I can still listen to Christian programs amid persecution."

* Not their real names to protect their privacy

"Give ear to my words,
O Lord, consider my groaning.
Heed the sound of my cry for help,
my King and my God,
For to You I pray."

– PSALM 5:1-2

14

Reaching Behind Closed Doors

ROI – RETURN on investment – is a widely used business metric. You measure the profitability of an investment by calculating its monetary value versus its cost. Let's say you invest $1,000 in a venture, but it makes $10,000. Your ROI would be 9, or 900%. That would be high indeed.

TWR President Lauren Libby expresses caution, however, especially if you misapply that concept to ministry.

Problems can possibly arise when it comes to donating toward a media outreach targeting reclusive regimes such as North Korea. The return on investment may remain elusive because listener responses from those secluded countries are ever so rare. So, would that represent a strong ROI or one that's overly risky?

"Frankly, I think there is an overemphasis on 'return on investment' in the Western church," Libby said in an interview with Andy Napier, the host and producer of *Footsteps*, a daily TWR program that airs on more than 220 stations in the U.S.

He explained that media organizations can conduct listener surveys in the U.S. or Europe to determine how many people are listening to a specific broadcast. But that can't be done in North Korea or elsewhere where governments keep their people insulated from the outside world.

"The world is becoming more and more of a closed place, and we have countries that are closing down, to Christians in particular," Libby said. "We know that believers are suffering. TWR is aware of this, and that's why we're actually expanding our programming to be able to reach people where they are with the hope of Jesus and to give them assurance of God's love and care."

Some people say shortwave radio is old, antiquated and overly costly. On the contrary, shortwave radio from TWR's shortwave station on the Pacific island of Guam remains critical to reaching this insulated region of the world, where persecution is on the rise.

"In the case of North Korea and others, we may never see the return on our investment until we get to heaven," the TWR president added. "But that won't keep us from investing our resources in helping to reach them with the gospel!"

Bicycles and motorbikes are common modes of transportation in the Vietnamese capital of Hanoi.

A TWR Korea staffer reads a letter brought out from North Korea for a TWR video. North Koreans listen to TWR broadcasts in secret. They send out letters at great risk.

When TWR teams do receive messages from these countries, they draw great encouragement and elicit heartfelt thanks to God for how he is moving even when human eyes can't detect his handiwork. Here is the story of Trinh* from Vietnam, followed by letter excerpts from listeners in North Korea.

WHEN TRINH WAS much younger, he wasn't just rich, he was loaded. He also had a legion of friends. Other Vietnamese looked to him and up to him.

But though wealthy and popular, Trinh had a false sense of security. He thought he was immune to difficulties. So he pursued anything and everything he wanted – with gusto – shrugging off the possibility he would suffer any consequences. Blinded by pride, Trinh made costly decisions. "My wealthy and satisfied lifestyle led me to many vices," he recalled. "I was recklessly extravagant."

Despite being married, he started sleeping with other women. He also became hooked on gambling, running up hefty debts.

"I was so indulgent until all my possessions were gone," he said.

Trinh's creditors hounded him. They wanted their money. "I had to sell everything I had," he admitted. "That included my house, car, land and farm. I ended in poverty."

But his troubles didn't end there. His wife and children abandoned him. His relatives and friends also turned their backs on him.

Trinh's world came crashing down on him, and he fell into a deep depression. "But to make matters even worse, I suffered a stroke, which led to the loss of both of my legs," he said. "I was paralyzed. I couldn't walk or do anything other than wait for death."

But he was not totally forgotten. Hearing about Trinh's plight, some Christians reached out to the then aging man. They invited him to church one Sunday. There he received an unexpected gift. "I got a radio from the church pastor so I could listen to programs from Trans World Radio," he said.

Those broadcasts from Guam fell on fertile spiritual ground.

"I heard about Jesus and accepted him as my Savior," Trinh declared. "God's words in the radio program, *The Word Today*, uplifted me. They touched my heart, and I sincerely repented of my sins."

God's Word transformed his life. He regretted the mistakes he had made so often earlier in life, but he knew that God had forgiven him and cleansed his sinful past. He looked forward to following and serving the Lord wholeheartedly.

"Although my health is failing and I am old, I know God will take care of me as I keep his words in my heart faithfully," Trinh said.

BECAUSE OF SEVERE persecution, North Korean Christians must live out their faith in secret. For many, the radio is the only way these believers receive biblical teaching and encouragement.

News reports indicate that North Koreans are not permitted to listen to foreign broadcasts, and radios are fixed-tuned to government stations.

But TWR's South Korean ministry team, with the help of other Christian organizations, has been able to quietly distribute tens of thousands of radios in North Korea over the past 20 years. They also produce programming for their persecuted brothers and sisters in the North, reaching out with Bible reading and teaching, seminary training, children's programs, and a worship service on the air. TWR's national partner in South Korea is also expanding its reach to refugees living outside the country, which is proving to be an effective way of encouraging them.

Here are letters they have received from listeners in North Korea, sometimes referred to as "the hermit kingdom." These letters have been sent at great personal risk.

- "Without your programs, love and dedication, we would not have access to the gospel of our Father in heaven, and we would be lost in darkness."

- "We could only keep our faith and live like children of God during hardships and fierce persecution because of the devotion of the TWR staff and the grace of our Lord Jesus Christ."

- "We are assisted and guided by the message of the gospel since we cannot gather together in one place for worship."

- "We have become regular listeners of the TWR program since you told us about it. We aim to pass on what we have heard from the program to our relatives."

- "Together, we raise our voices in worship when the radio plays hymns, and we draw near to God when we listen to the messages."

- "I have no words to express our gratitude after receiving your precious and warm, loving support. We pray that faith, hope and love will be with all the brothers and sisters around the world."

* Not his real name to protect his privacy

SECTION IV

Catching New Waves

TWR IS CONSTANTLY asking the Lord to open doors to declare God's truth to those people still unreached and to provide improved ways to minister to existing audiences. Sometimes we zero in on a specific people group or focus on a smaller audience within a much larger one. And then we come up with just the right medium to reach them with the gospel or touch their lives with the right message from God's Word. And if a crisis erupts on the global stage and a glaring need surfaces, we don't hesitate to respond with the compassion of Jesus Christ. We stand ready to press ahead when the Lord prompts us to jump into action.

"Many, O Lord my God, are the wonders which You have done, and Your thoughts toward us; there is none to compare with You. If I would declare and speak of them, they would be too numerous to count."

— PSALM 40:5

15

Bringing Light to Women

L YING ON HER bed in an isolated corner of a hospital ward in North Africa, Aafana* kept smiling at other patients and toward those taking care of her. She couldn't help herself. She wanted them to know that, despite her pain, God was in control of her life – and her future – and that they, too, could trust him.

Aafana's calm – even joy-filled – demeanor belied the catastrophic circumstances that required her to check into this crowded hospital. COVID-19 was ravaging her body.

She knew her time on earth would soon end. Yet peace surrounded her. And her imminent death could not stop her from continuing to serve her Lord, the same one who had saved her so many years before. In fact, she reached out with a greater sense of urgency to as many people in the hospital as possible, telling them about God's unfailing love in Jesus Christ.

Through TWR's *Women of Hope* radio program, Aafana had heard the wonderful news that God loved her. That message, describing Jesus' death on a cross for her sins, touched her heart – forever. When she heard that

* Not her real name to protect her privacy

141

day that she could be eternally forgiven if she trusted in Jesus Christ as her Savior, she didn't hesitate to pray to accept Christ into her heart.

After surrendering her life to Christ, she stayed in touch with the TWR Women of Hope team. Her contacts were so frequent, the staff "joked that she may have had one team member on speed dial!"

When Aafana first showed symptoms of COVID-19, she didn't think much of it. But as she steadily declined, her family became alarmed and took her to the hospital. However, it was short of equipment, including oxygen tanks, as well as proper medication. As a result, Aafana was placed in the corner of a ward, "more or less just hoping for the best."

That's when the same message that she had heard and embraced years before compelled Aafana, despite her failing health, to demonstrate Christ's love and grace to fellow patients.

TWR Women of Hope team members tried to visit Aafana but were turned away. They were able to connect with her by phone, however, texting her frequently. She said she was asked multiple times why she kept smiling.

"Don't you know your spot is the 'death spot'?" they asked rather morosely, then derisively.

She kept smiling. "I know where I am going. Follow Jesus!"

One of Aafana's texts read, "I am still telling everyone here about JESUS!"

Then communication stopped. No more replies. Aafana's brother rushed to the hospital and had to force his way in to check on her. He found her still lying in that corner, but she had died.

"She kept talking about salvation in Jesus Christ till the very end," the other patients told him. "She peacefully passed away."

In reflecting upon Aafana's life – and death – one Women of Hope team member said, "What an amazing testimony of hope – even assurance in Christ. Only Jesus can put a smile on our face in dire circumstances. What a friend we have!"

THE *WOMEN OF HOPE* broadcast was launched in 1997. It was the centerpiece of an essentially two-pronged worldwide outreach to women and known originally as Project Hannah – named for the mother of Samuel in the Bible. Prayer was the other primary component of this fledgling ministry. Marli Spieker was its founder.

Spieker had been waiting on God for her next ministry focus. An energetic doer, she was becoming antsy. But deep down, she knew God would show her in his perfect timing. She and her TWR missionary husband, Edmund, were in Singapore, so while he was tied up in meetings, she ventured out by bus to enjoy the colorful cultures on display in the heart of downtown.

While there, she had to make a quick phone call, so she stepped into a phone booth in a nearby shopping center. What happened next changed her life – and ministry thrust.

The automatic door next to the phone booth opened, and a young couple strolled in. In the stifling heat, the man was dressed in a comfortable cotton T-shirt. The woman, on the other hand, wore a black head-to-toe burqa, with only a little net peephole for her eyes.

Spieker stared, first stunned, then grieved. "God! How can this be?"

She sensed God replying: "Did you see that black veil? It is not only over her head, but also over her mind, her heart, her family, her spirit – her whole life! This woman lives in darkness!"

"What would you have me do to bring her into your light? Show me, and I'll do it."

Spieker's mind reverted to Exodus 4, the Scripture in which God asked Moses what he had in his hand and Moses answered that it was his shepherd's rod. She believed God was asking her a similar question: "What is the closest thing available to you? What do you have in your hand?"

"A microphone. Radio. Trans World Radio."

"I knew the power of radio!" Spieker wrote in her book *When Hope Wins.* "Its waves can go where missionaries can't! It penetrates any man-made barrier, whether geographical, political, ideological or religious. And even today, radio continues to be a very effective mass-media tool!"

Spieker and the media ministry she served yielded that platform to God, and he paved the way for Project Hannah's debut on a global stage and scale.

RADIO BROADCASTS AND prayer remain bedrock components of this ministry, now known as TWR Women of Hope. The *Women of Hope* radio program is available in 70-plus languages, and prayer intercessors in 125 countries, who receive prayer calendars each month translated in their heart languages, keep the work before the throne of God.

The program has powerful effects.

A 15-year-old listener to *Women of Hope* from Nepal wrote that her family's religion made it hard for her to follow Jesus, but that the radio programs had changed her thinking and attitude toward Christianity.

Women and girls gather at a Project Hannah event in Cambodia in 2009.

"Please pray for me that one day I may come to know Jesus," she wrote.

But TWR Women of Hope's leadership knows the ministry must continue to both evolve and expand to stay current and germane in an ever-changing world. More than 500 volunteers are now teaming with TWR Women of Hope staff to bolster its effectiveness.

Many wonderful new digital and audio programs that are of varying lengths and relevant to multiple cultures have been written by teams on the ground to address issues women face every day.

"If you're going to influence culture, you've got to influence both women and men," said TWR President Lauren Libby. "It's amazing to see how God is using our TWR Women of Hope ministry to transform the hearts and lives of so many women from around the world."

One new program that's being developed is called *Precious and Beloved*. It's especially designed for women in the Muslim world. Scripts focus on bringing the hope of Jesus in a way that is relatable and that can be understood and embraced. Developers completed 52 magazine-style programs in 2023.

Beyond programming, global events are also springing up to bring awareness and forge partnerships with churches. A ministry to survivors of human sex trafficking has been introduced. It features an audio and video drama comprising 11 episodes telling real stories of real women who have come to know Jesus. The next generation of TWR Women of Hope leaders is also being trained. And certainly, TWR Women of Hope is taking advantage of a burgeoning social media presence among 750,000 followers to increase exposure and to lay the groundwork for stronger connections.

Women are asking questions about a host of issues, from identity to trauma and from God to faith. They yearn to know that they have value and purpose – and that they're loved. Through emails and other social media connections, TWR Women of Hope regional and local teams are building conversations with those seekers. TWR Women of Hope has become a safe place for them to ask their questions and, through the power of the Holy Spirit, many of these women have come to know Christ!

Spieker passed the leadership baton to Dr. Peggy Banks in 2016. When

Banks moved on to another ministry at the end of 2022, Susie Pek became the third global leader of TWR Women of Hope. A Brazilian like Spieker, Pek previously had served as TWR Women of Hope coordinator for Latin America and the Caribbean.

"She's uniquely gifted for this role," Libby said when he announced the appointment. "She brings an international perspective and a wealth of experience."

Pek was already the presenter of *Women of Hope, Did you Know* and *Audio Prayer Calendar* in Portuguese. She has ministered to women all over Brazil in retreats, conferences and church events.

Pek lives in São Paulo with her husband, Douglas Pek, a minister of administration at Calvary International Church. In her first year, as Pek got to know TWR Women of Hope staff and volunteers around the world, the ministry she led was focused on producing *Precious and Beloved* as well as *Hidden Treasures Part 2*, the working title for a new set of the programs focused on the gospel's answers to human trafficking.

Susie Pek became the third director of TWR Women of Hope in 2023.

Marli Spieker (left), the founder of what is now known as TWR Women of Hope, confers with her successor, Dr. Peggy Banks. The ministry was originally known as Project Hannah, after the biblical mother of Samuel.

"I love the foundation that Marli laid," Pek said. "I think it was a very solid foundation. And I love what Peggy has done building on that foundation."

If Spieker's main emphasis was on prayer and Banks' on leadership development, Pek said she's especially devoted to teaching and equipping. But all the emphases work together in one ministry.

"And it is my desire that women around the world and across generations find this hope in Jesus, that they find healing, that they know we can have life eternal and abundant life because of Christ despite our circumstances," Pek said. "And it's real. Relationship with Christ transforms us and transforms our lives, and I just pray that I'll be able to communicate that message very clearly."

"Who is like the Lord our God, who is enthroned on high, who humbles Himself to behold the things that are in heaven and in the earth? He raises the poor from the dust and lifts the needy from the ash heap, to make them sit with princes, with the princes of His people."

— PSALM 113:5-8

16

Compassion Extended
to the Roma People

RENATUS CZESKLEBA ANSWERED the doorbell at his home in southern Austria on a Saturday night. The precise date is unknown, but it would have been in the late 1970s or early 1980s, according to Werner Kroemer, who heard Czeskleba's story later.

Czeskleba, a German-born church planter who is now deceased, knew at a glance the two men facing him were Roma.

"What do you want?" Czeskleba asked.

"We want some wine. Not very much; perhaps half a bottle."

"What do you need the wine for?"

"Tomorrow is Sunday. And we want to celebrate the Lord's Supper. And we have no wine."

Czeskleba told him that a small group would gather at his house to worship in the morning. Perhaps they could come, and all could celebrate the Lord's Supper together.

The next morning, they came: 16 Roma people, including children. They all celebrated the Lord's Supper, and Czeskleba invited the Roma to come again the following Sunday.

The leader of the group looked sadly at him and said, "We would very much like to come, but we are not wanted here [in this region]. We have to move on."

Kroemer couldn't get that story out of his head after Czeskleba told him about it in the late 1980s. In 1994, when Kroemer was named European director for TWR, he realized it was part of his responsibility to do something on behalf of Europe's Roma people. In answering his prayers and those of many others, the Lord Jesus orchestrated a meeting on the other side of the globe to begin a ministry that continues to gain momentum today.

FORMERLY KNOWN BY the sometimes-disparaging term "Gypsies," the Roma people are one of the most discriminated-against and disadvantaged groups in Europe, according to the human rights-focused Council of Europe. At between 10 million and 12 million, they compose the largest minority group in Europe. More than half a million Roma died in Nazi concentration camps, according to the council.

It's believed that the Roma people began migrating from northern India to Europe more than a thousand years ago, according to the human-rights organization Amnesty International. Although they were traditionally nomadic, most now stay in one place.

Millions of Roma live in poverty, according to Amnesty, and many live under the threat of eviction, police harassment and violent attacks. Their children often are taught in segregated schools and receive less education.

They are finding faith in Jesus Christ in increasing numbers, running against the current of European culture, Kroemer said.

"On this continent, evangelical churches are declining," he said. "There's hardly any increase. And for years, especially the first decade of 2000-2010, there [have been] just two exceptions, really. One was Ukraine. And the other was the Roma."

·||||·

KROEMER HAD THE longing to bring radio programming to the Roma, but he didn't have the resources. In 1995, he attended a global evangelism conference in South Korea. Before flying there, he prayed that the Lord would put him in contact with someone who could start a Roma program.

On the last evening of the conference, Kroemer was sitting in the last row of a hall, wondering why God hadn't answered his prayer.

"And while I was sitting there, a nice gentleman, unknown to me, took a seat beside me, and asked, 'Brother, what burdens you so much?'" Kroemer related.

Somewhat reluctantly, Kroemer explained his vision for a radio program for the Roma. As soon as he was done, the man offered $40,000 in support on behalf of the U.S. organization he was serving with as president, Words of Hope.

For those wishing to reach and disciple the Roma, the language is challenging. Kroemer explained that the Romani language (the language spoken by most of the Roma in Europe) has a simplified vocabulary comprising only about 30% of the words most Roma speak. The rest come from the languages of their host country. Roma have no homeland of their own, and those of them speaking Romani are widespread in about a dozen European countries.

"And so you have lots of different Romani dialects based on where they are living," Kroemer said.

The programs in cooperation with Words of Hope were in Balkan Romani and resulted in a number of churches being founded in Bulgaria. To reach the Roma in Romania, *Thru the Bible* programs were produced and broadcast in Romani Kalderash.

TWR added broadcasting in Romani dialects used by larger concentrations of Roma people. By 2010, two programs were being recorded in the Romani language in Serbia: *Shalom Romalen* (*Peace to the Roma*) and *Romana Krio* (*Voice of the Roma*). Since 2007, *Voice of Truth* has been aired for the benefit of the Roma population of Prilep in Macedonia. Another TWR program, *Roma Camp Moves On*, ministered to Roma people in Ukraine.

AS EVANGELISM TO the Roma continues, TWR participates in the next step as well.

"I asked [Roma ministry leaders] what is the thing that you think is important for Roma? How can we help you?" recalled Samuel Lacho, TWR director for Central and Eastern Europe. "And they said that they are really missing a discipleship program."

Lacho joined the TWR team in 2017 in Bratislava, Slovakia, after many years of developing Christian ministries elsewhere. Soon after, he went with a Roma pastor to a nearby village where he was planting a church.

"I actually realized that people were living on a dirt floor, a whole family in one room," Lacho said. "And at the same time, when they sang songs to God, they sang wholeheartedly, and it was so beautiful that I actually brought my whole family [the next time]," he said.

Roma people embrace religion and get excited when they hear the gospel, Lacho said. But it's a smaller number of Roma who will let "the kingdom-of-God culture infiltrate their Roma culture or transform their Roma culture and really heal it, I would say. You don't have to change it, but it's just healed."

Any culture of the world clashes with the culture of the gospel, Lacho said.

Kroemer told of a Roma church that grew in a Bulgarian ghetto. Before beginning a year of education to receive baptism, prospective members had to give up stealing, smoking, drinking, beating their wives and wearing a knife. After a year, the church's elders would check with the individual's unbelieving neighbors to see if they had noticed a change in behavior. The baptism would take place only if those neighbors confirmed the change.

From the time Werner Kroemer obtained funding, TWR moved to get the Word of God into the hearts of Roma people. Here, Roma women worship the Lord at a 2022 TWR Women of Hope gathering in Sofia, Bulgaria.

The gospel has dramatically changed the Roma culture, particularly in northern Bulgaria, said Lauren Libby, president of TWR. He told of visiting a concrete-block home there that was about 12 feet by 12 feet with a tin roof and containing a bed, water pipes, a hammock in which a baby slept, a potbellied stove and a radio.

A Roma man there told Libby that he had been challenged by the gospel to stop beating his wife, and several other men had been challenged not to steal. "Now you have to realize that one of the primary economic drivers of the Roma communities is theft," Libby said. "And so rather than do that, they went out and bought a back-end loader, and they began to dig foundations for houses. So they shifted from stealing to building foundations."

Stoyko Petkov, CEO of TWR's partner in Bulgaria, Studio 865, has been instrumental in developing outreach to the Roma.

"And you know what? God was using that in a phenomenal way," Libby said. "And because of the vision of Kroemer and Petkov, they have begun to influence the whole culture in northern Bulgaria and southern Romania."

To help meet the need to infiltrate the Roma culture, TWR's ministry to the Roma developed *The Roma Discipleship Tool* for Central and East Europe. By 2023, 32 of the envisioned 52 programs had been produced in the Serbian language, which is accessible to most of the Roma people of that country, Lacho said. It's also being developed in English because of the availability of Roma producers in Serbia who speak English.

Roma pastors produce programs for Roma people and address topics that are relevant to the Roma, such as witchcraft and thinking about what the future holds, Lacho said.

The pastors balked at writing scripts for the programs, he said. "So we decided to go totally on an oral route. And so we prepared the script in such a way that when we sit down together with the producers, we just talk. We just talk for two hours, and I'm the only one who writes things down."

The result is a 30-minute program consisting of three seven-minute segments interspersed with songs. They are posted on social media because most of the Roma people, though poor, have cell phones and internet access.

As this book was being completed, work was underway with three Roma leaders for a Romanian version of the discipleship tool. Serbian producers were starting on a children's program with biblical animation and original Roma songs. Another effort, geared toward Roma Bulgarian women, was in the early phases.

Although many Roma people are illiterate, some have responded gratefully to the programming. A Roma couple who lives in the city of Pančevo, Serbia, with their nine children reported listening regularly to *Thru the Bible.*

"Although we had a lot of worries and problems, God restored our strength and gave us new faith through this program," they wrote. "We had peace in our hearts that everything would be fine. And so it was. ... Sometimes our neighbors [come to] our house because they are interested in why we are so different from them."

"Praise the Lord! How blessed is the man who fears the Lord,
who greatly delights in His commandments."

– PSALM 112:1

17

Men of Valor and Courage

AFTER THREE DECADES of men's ministry, Lonnie Berger was seeing little fruit.

He struggled over 1 Corinthians 3:10, in which the apostle Paul said, "Like a skilled master builder I laid a foundation."

"And I began to think, 'Well, man, how am I building?'" Berger recalled. "What am I building?"

Berger's reflections led to a new approach to men's ministry that now is embodied in Every Man A Warrior (EMAW), one of two ministries in the TWR world specifically geared toward men.

Berger formed EMAW in 2011 as a ministry of The Navigators, which is still a partner in the work. The approach he takes comes out of his conclusion that men were being taught the Scriptures but not why they mattered.

"I'll go to a Bible study, and I'll say, 'Now men, we're going to study the Bible, and we're going to help you get to know God,'" Berger said of the former

Lonnie Berger founded Every Man A Warrior in 2011. It has been a ministry within TWR since 2017.

approach. "Well, men go, 'OK, I've done stuff like that, and it's been boring and irrelevant.'

"But if I go to a group and say, 'Men, we're going to study money, marriage, raising children, sex, work and getting through hard times. Do any of you struggle with these issues?' And, you know, everybody raises their hands."

The curriculum he developed – three books, 28 lessons over 32 weeks – focuses on just those sorts of issues. But the men who participate are immersed in Scripture. At the end of the 32 weeks, they will have learned and meditated on 31 Bible verses.

Men have responded. When he launched EMAW and its three texts, a Christian publisher told Berger that he would be doing well to sell 20,000 copies in his lifetime. Women will buy discipleship material, the publisher said; men won't.

In fact, 25,000 copies sold in the first two years.

EMAW'S ENTRY INTO the TWR realm in 2017 marked the increasing globalization of the men's ministry. "I think that was a blessing, because what it did was it gave an international platform for Every Man A Warrior," said TWR President Lauren Libby, a steadfast supporter of EMAW from the outset.

By late 2023, more than 250,000 EMAW books had been sold. EMAW groups had been established in all 50 U.S. states and in more than 50 countries, with key leaders in 40 countries. The book had been translated into 25 languages.

In the summer of 2022, Berger appointed five men to lead the work of EMAW in the U.S. so he could devote 80% of his time to the international ministry.

The work is growing rapidly. More than 60,000 men have taken part in the United States and more than 17,000 in Brazil, according to Berger. Europe has 200 groups in 17 countries. EMAW groups are established in 16 African nations, and more than 100 groups have been set up in Taiwan and China.

In Kenya, EMAW has been invited into all 125 prisons, and 125 prison chaplains have been trained to lead EMAW groups. At least 1,250 inmates had come to faith in Christ as of late 2023, and more than 2,500 inmates were in the EMAW curriculum.

Libby has witnessed the difference EMAW makes in the lives of families. "I have talked to women whose husbands have been involved in Every Man A Warrior," he said. "And invariably what they will say is: As my husband began to get into Scriptures and began to pray and began to engage with our family, there was a total cultural change."

Berger believes praying women are the force behind EMAW.

"Women have prayed the Every Man A Warrior ministry into being," Berger said. "If I heard the Lord right, God said, 'Millions of Christian women have been praying for decades, "God, please help the men. Help them be better husbands, better fathers and the spiritual leaders of the home.""

Inmates display their EMAW materials in a Kenyan prison. As of late 2023, at least 1,250 inmates had come to faith in Christ through the program.

EMAW IS AN international ministry that began in response to the need that Berger saw in the United States. *Men of Courage* is a ministry that began in response to a need in the Muslim world.

Caleb Petersen's* assignment when he joined TWR in early 2020 was no biggie: "So, welcome. [Now] we want you to produce a strategy for reaching the Muslims all over Europe," he was told. Petersen related that audacious challenge with a smile on his face and a twinkle in his eye.

He was new to TWR but not a novice at the work. He and his family had served as missionaries in Türkiye for four years, and he already was serving with related ministries. He still is.

Petersen soon came to two conclusions: First, a key need was to reach Muslim men. Second, no programs existed to do so.

With support of TWR leadership, Petersen began working to fill that gap, consulting Muslim-background believers and other experts from different parts of the world. His question: What 20 to 25 topics would be of interest to all Muslim men? Topics emerged such as forgiveness, lying, fatherhood, relationships and identity.

The first plan was to develop programs in European Arabic, Petersen said. But no one was available with both the background and the time to spearhead the project. Instead, God led Petersen to Türkiye, where he already had relationships because of his four years there. Concepts for a script grew out of discussions among four men who were Muslim-background believers. A Turkish woman with a journalistic background was chosen to write the scripts.

Men of Courage is not a traditional project, Petersen said. Each episode is presented in three versions: an "appetizer" of 10 to 30 seconds good for social media; a two- to three-minute audio drama; and a program of 15 to 30 minutes in which men will discuss the topic.

A pilot program was aired in Türkiye in 2022, and a full first season of 52 episodes began in 2023. It made sense to start in Türkiye, Petersen said, not only because that nation has a large Muslim population but also because he had previously served in Türkiye and had a trust relationship built. Pro-

Kenyan prison inmates study the
Every Man A Warrior curriculum.
By 2024, EMAW had been invited
into all 125 Kenyan prisons.

grams for other nations are under development. The goal is to address the same topics in other places and other languages but not in exactly the same way.

"We don't want to have a set script that we are just translating into different languages, because there are differences in cultures on a deep level," Petersen said.

The short drama is the core program, Petersen said. The approach is "pre-evangelistic." He expects the initial audience to have little interest in Christianity, so the drama will be used to prepare the ground for evangelism down the road.

"I see it as a journey from not knowing Christ, even maybe [being] hostile ... to [being] more interested, curious, interacting with people, then making a decision and coming to Christ," Petersen said. "My vision is really that we need to provide content on each of these stages along the journey."

THE APPROACHES AND the audiences are different, but both EMAW and *Men of Courage* have an underlying purpose.

"I think we'll have a greater impact to change a nation for Christ when we preach the gospel but we also disciple the men," Berger said. "When we do both, I think we're more effective."

* *A pseudonym is used for security reasons.*

"God be gracious to us and bless us, and cause His face to shine upon us—that Your way may be known on the earth, Your salvation among all nations."

— PSALM 67:1-2

18

A Unique Opportunity in Southeast Asia

JASON* AND EMMA* climb into their car for their regular 40-minute morning commute from their home to their respective offices. Jason works in a government facility, while Emma is in the banking industry.

As they do every day, they turn on the radio, already tuned to BE 107 FM. Their favorite program is *Turning Point* with California pastor David Jeremiah because it provides biblical instruction for living with hope.

"His broadcast gives us insights into how to deal with life issues and challenges," Jason said.

But there's an added benefit to listening to Dr. Jeremiah each morning. "We get to learn English from the program," Jason noted. "That's a great bonus."

Turning Point is one of several English-language broadcasts that make up BE 107's *Morning Buzz* lineup. They have an avid listenership.

* *Not their real names to protect their privacy or for security reasons*

That also includes Vanessa.* She's a dentist, who opened a clinic in one of the many malls in Batam – the largest city in the Riau Islands, Indonesia. She, too, has a long commute to her workplace.

"*Morning Buzz* is my friend on my way to work," Vanessa said. "I feel so blessed with the songs I can listen to. I sing along and sense the Holy Spirit speaking to me through the words."

There are so many more Jasons and Emmas and Vanessas. For BE 107 FM represents an engaging opportunity to instruct and inspire a potential audience of 7 million people across the surrounding islands and nations of the Singapore Strait.

GOD OPENED THIS incredible window for ministry partnership within the region. On July 1, 2021, BE 107 FM became associated with TWR's network of affiliate stations.

TWR provides it with daily programs that feature a broad selection of Indonesian- and English-language contemporary music, short features and programming aimed at uplifting listeners with good news. What's particularly helpful is that the Indonesian language, which is a dialect of Standard Malay, is generally understood by Malaysians.

In addition to *Turning Point*, other teaching programs include Tony Evans' *The Urban Alternative* and Ron Hutchcraft's *A Word With You*. They round out a four-hour morning block of English programs and contemporary Christian music hosted by Daren Tan. English is widely spoken in Singapore and many parts of the region. On Saturdays and Sundays, *Bold Steps* with Mark Jobe, president of Moody Bible Institute, is aired.

Content will expand further as similar cooperating media ministries and local partner organizations add their broadcasts to the schedule.

TWR has had a long history of broadcasting to Asia via its powerful shortwave station KTWR on the Pacific Island of Guam. "We can reach farther and cover greater amounts of terrain from KTWR," said Daryl Renshaw, TWR's international vice president for Asia. "And we're called to minister to cultures where it's not feasible to implement a community

* *Not their real names to protect their privacy or for security reasons*

164

radio station. So KTWR will continue to be relevant for reaching people in closed countries like North Korea or restricted countries becoming more like closed countries such as China."

But now, BE 107 FM offers the extraordinary opportunity to have a different kind of impact among its audience.

"Stations like BE 107 FM are personable and can have a personal touch on their audiences because the staff live among their listeners, and in some cases listeners can literally reach out and touch them at live local events promoting the station," Renshaw added. "So BE 107 is unique, and we're tremendously honored to be a part of what God is doing there. We look forward to seeing what kind of ongoing impact it will have in the future."

BELOW: A woman is seen on the island city-state of Singapore, which has a population of close to 6 million people. BE 107 FM brings the hope of Christ to Singapore from outside its borders.

ABOVE: BE 107 FM is located on the Indonesian island of Batam. Its affiliation with TWR dates from July 1, 2021.

Three Malaysian women show varying expressions as they look at the camera. The Indonesian language in which BE 107 FM broadcasts is generally understood by Malaysians.

ALMOST 19% OF Singapore's nearly 6 million people are Christians – or nearly 1.15 million. One of the many strengths of the church in Singapore is that so many of its members have a heart and a burden for people who don't yet know Jesus, said Eugene Lim, who lives in the city-state. He serves as TWR's point person for resource development of projects and ministries in Asia.

"The church in Singapore is mission-minded," he said. "They send missionaries all over Asia and to other continents. So we want to encourage them to be even more missional and even more committed to the calling that God has put into their hearts. That's why we're making sure we have solid discipleship programs every day."

But a major hurdle had to be overcome to begin to reach and encourage them. "In Singapore, we have Muslims, Hindus, Buddhists, Christians and other religions," Lim said.

He said people can gain access to both local and overseas mainstream Christian programming through the internet. "But since the Singapore government has a policy of multiracial tolerance and multireligious tolerance, to maintain harmony among the races and the religions, it has instituted a regulation that says there should not be religious broadcasts of any kind over local radio in Singapore itself," he explained.

With BE 107 FM being located outside of Singapore's borders in nearby Indonesia, that stipulation has been satisfied. And the Indonesian government permits this.

This program affiliation with BE 107 FM excites Daniel Saputra,* TWR's international director for Southeast Asia. "When we say we are reaching people in the region, we are not reaching some homogeneous group of people," he said. "There are so many different ethnic groups that speak different languages living all over Singapore, Malaysia and the surrounding Indonesian islands."

From the outset, the reaction has been positive. One listener sent an email to the morning show's host. "I want to take this opportunity to thank you and the team for the work of BE 107 FM. My family listens to you every morning when we can, and we actively tell our friends. It's a privilege to listen to a radio station that broadcasts Christian programming in Singapore."

JUST AS CHRISTIANS in Singapore were burdened to broadcast to their country, Saputra was already exploring avenues to connect with the people of southern Malaysia (the Malay Peninsula portion of Malaysia) as well as the people in northern Indonesia.

The Lord paved the way for Batam. "Things lined up that I can only attribute to God," Renshaw said.

The station allows TWR to proclaim biblical truth to people who have not heard about Jesus Christ. And people are listening.

"TWR is bringing hope to people who are living in challenging circumstances who would never darken the doors of a church," Renshaw said. "Not because they would be averse to it, but because they haven't been invited or they might not feel welcome. So the broadcasts on BE 107 are able to speak to them about spiritual issues."

GOD'S PROVISION HAS been inspiring and cascading. People from around the world are rallying around the Batam station's mission. And they're giving generously, ensuring that life-changing ministry would indeed get on the air.

After hearing about the station during a meeting, one gentleman looked squarely into the eyes of his colleagues and urged them to get behind it. "Why would we not do this?" he asked them. But his challenge wasn't just words. He gave $100,000 to help make ministry possible.

God touched the hearts of a couple who had inquired about how they might help through their personal giving. The husband and wife listened intently to multiple options. A campaign had begun to help meet the ministry needs of BE 107 FM, and the station and its potential impact especially piqued their interest. "We'll go home and pray about this," they said. The Lord moved deeply within them overnight. They called back the next day and said they would like to pick up a sizable amount of the ministry costs. They responded to God's promptings.

Indonesia's central and provincial government certainly has recognized what BE 107 FM has done for the community and how its programming is helping people with daily life. "The station received an award for its strong support to their drug-enforcement agency in making people aware of specific drugs that were coming in and the damage they can do to people," Renshaw said. "This has elicited positive attention to the station, and that's always great publicity that can draw more people to its programming."

The future looks bright, Renshaw said. "Not only am I encouraged by the station's vision for ministry, I'm encouraged by the participation of our younger workers in this," he said. "Most of them appear to be in their 20s and 30s. Sometimes people think of radio as a tool for the older generation. That's not evident by who's involved with BE 107 FM. They are our future, and we'll be able to hand it over to people who are talented, capable and committed. For that I'm thankful."

"Offer to God a sacrifice of thanksgiving and pay your vows to the Most High; Call upon Me in the day of trouble; I shall rescue you, and you will honor Me."

— PSALM 50:14-15

19

Expanding Commitment
to the Horn of Africa

T HEIR MARRIAGE CRUMBLING, Adane* and Eleni* sat across from each other, yet staring in opposite directions.

"Can't we find a way to reconcile?" Adane finally pleaded with his wife.

"No. I want a divorce," Eleni said. Her adamant reply stung.

The two ended their marriage in a local court and separated.

A year later, Adane slumped in a chair at his home in Ethiopia, lonely. He turned on his radio to fill the air with noise. The program startled him. It was in Amharic, his language.

What are these words? he wondered.

* Not their real names to protect their privacy

"You can know the living God and develop a personal relationship with him. Have your sins forgiven through faith in his Son, Jesus Christ. Put your trust in him and experience a new beginning."

A new beginning, Adane pondered. He bowed his head and surrendered his life to Jesus.

With hope in his heart, Adane called Eleni and invited her to listen to the program with him. Initially reluctant, she still agreed. As they heard the Bible explained, they discovered how these lessons could apply to daily life.

Can our marriage possibly be saved?

"The *Thru the Bible* program radically changed my life," Adane said. "Then Eleni and I believed God could help us solve our problems."

The couple put faith into action and renewed their marriage vows, this time in an evangelical church. "Now we're very happy," Adane said. "God bless you."

An Ethiopian woman holds her son in this 2010 photo. TWR is expanding its programming to Ethiopia and the rest of the Horn of Africa.

This heartwarming story of redemption and renewal is one of thousands that TWR staff have heard from listeners in the Horn of Africa. Burdened for people living throughout this region, TWR is expanding its programming to Ethiopia, Eritrea, Somalia, Sudan and South Sudan. Two hundred million people live in this spiritually closed part of the world, 80 million of whom are considered unreached.

Yet the hunger is there! "We need to address it," said TWR President Lauren Libby. "TWR has the capability to touch this troubled part of

A rural Ethiopian family displays their radio. Christ-centered radio touches the lives of families isolated in hard-to-reach areas of the Ethiopian countryside.

the world, which has certainly known war and resistance to the gospel. We're praying for more opportunities to make an impact in the lives of people. They really need Jesus."

Since many do not have access to the internet, a digital presence is limited, if not nonexistent. So TWR's broadcast site in the Kingdom of Eswatini, formerly known as Swaziland, is playing a key role in this ramped-up ministry focus. Additional programs will be beamed from this facility.

HEARTWARMING STORIES OF faith always keep the TWR team energized. Like that of Beza* and Naomi.* As college classmates in northeast Africa, they spent a lot of time together enjoying each other's company as well as studying. Their abiding friendship helped save Beza's life – physically and spiritually.

* Not their real names to protect their privacy

Beza comes from a Muslim background. She was forbidden to listen to anything – or anyone – concerning Christianity. But after meeting Naomi, a Christian, and getting to know her, Beza was willing to take the risk. And so was Naomi.

"Naomi is very honest and trustworthy," Beza said of her friend.

One day recently, Beza had a terrible headache. Soon she began vomiting. Naomi took Beza to a clinic, but unfortunately it was closed because of a public holiday. So she took her back to her dorm room.

Naomi then demonstrated her Christian love for her friend when she knelt and started praying for her. Rising to her feet, Naomi looked at her watch. It was almost 8 p.m. She asked Beza if she would like to listen to a Christian radio program called *Hope for Today*. It's produced by Heralds of Hope and broadcast by TWR. The program airs in the Amharic language, spoken in this region of Africa, including the country of Ethiopia.

Naomi told Beza she would be encouraged by its biblical teaching. Beza agreed to listen.

That night, the topic of the program was about the woman who had been bleeding for 12 years but no one was able to heal her. Beza listened closely as she heard how the woman approached Jesus from behind and touched the edge of his cloak. Immediately her bleeding stopped. Jesus asked who touched him, and the woman fell at his feet, trembling. Jesus said to her, "Daughter, your faith has made you well; go in peace" (Luke 8:48, NASB).

When the radio program was over, Naomi again prayed for Beza. "That evening, I got free from my suffering and pain," Beza said.

But that wasn't all! Beza was also freed from the bondage of her sin as she turned to Jesus Christ and prayed to receive him as her personal Savior.

"I praise God for he saved me through the Heralds of Hope radio program," Beza told us in a telephone call.

NOT ONLY IS Christ-centered radio reaching college classmates, but it's also touching the lives of families isolated in hard-to-reach areas of the vast Ethiopian countryside.

Eyasu* and his family used to reside in the southern part of the country, where many Christians live. A few of those believers had to move to a different, quite remote section of the country to find work. There is no formal church in that area.

But Eyasu and his wife and their children – along with neighbors – gather each week around the radio and listen to the *Hope for Today* program.

"We are always in anticipation waiting for your program to start," Eyasu said. "We listen to the Word of God and get encouraged!"

Heralds of Hope also airs its *Hope for Today* program in Oromo, another language spoken in northeast Africa. It, too, is broadcast by TWR. It's making a lasting difference in the lives of those listeners who depend upon it for teaching that is faithful to the Scriptures.

"I am an elder in a church, and we listen together as a family to this program," one listener told TWR. "We always invite people to join us in listening. It strengthens our faith."

Another listener said, "We like listening to this program in the morning at breakfast time. It makes a great start to our day."

Then this listener encouraged TWR staff and the program producers. "We are always praying for you, that God will provide you more wisdom to produce good programs!"

"The Lord sustains all who fall and raises up all who are bowed down. The eyes of all look to You, and You give them their food in due time. You open Your hand and satisfy the desire of every living thing."

— PSALM 145:14-15

20

Running Toward
Humanitarian Crises

B BC REPORTER MICHAEL Buerk called it a "biblical famine."

The food crisis that hit Ethiopia from 1983-85 caused an estimated 1 million deaths, according to the United Nations. When Buerk's reporting brought the famine to Western television screens in October 1984, it elicited horror – and action. It spurred the hit singles "We Are the World" and "Do They Know It's Christmas?" and led to the multivenue Live Aid "super concert" that raised $127 million for African famine relief.

Many traveled to the Horn of Africa to see for themselves – and to help. Among them was Paul Freed, TWR's founder. It added to his perspective on the ministry's role.

"He was convinced that it was not enough for Trans World Radio to only broadcast teaching and preaching of the gospel programs but that it was time that the ministry started programs on matters that affected people's daily lives," said Bernice Gatere, longtime director of TWR Kenya.

TWR's mission is to share Christ with the world through mass media so that lasting fruit is produced. Humanitarian work isn't specifically within that calling. Yet as Christ followers, TWR can't help but respond to the glaring needs across the globe. That often means being involved with or starting a crisis response, then handing over the work to another agency.

TWR partners and associated ministries have pitched in, for example, following deadly earthquakes in Haiti in 2021 and in Türkiye and Syria as well as Morocco in 2023; and catastrophic flooding in Pakistan in 2022. Especially in Africa, though, TWR and its partners have been the hands and feet of Jesus to people in desperate need.

That's because what they need most is Jesus, said Lauren Libby, president of TWR.

"Food provides sustenance for a period of time," he said. "Political situations change dramatically, but the kingdom of God never changes, and it is the only true source of hope. And so that's why when we get into a crisis situation, that's why it's important to be there."

The initiative that grew out of Paul Freed's concern first was known as Save a Generation before being renamed Africa Challenge in 1986. Gatere began her TWR career as a scriptwriter for *Africa Challenge* radio programs that focused on topics such as growing and storing grain, health, family and lifestyles.

RADIO BROADCASTS WERE an essential part of the initiative. But hands-on efforts took place as well. In 1995, TWR contributed solar box cookers to the massive Kakuma Refugee Camp in northwestern Kenya. The camp, which held more than 150,000 refugees by 2021, was formed in 1992 to house the "lost boys of Sudan," children who had been displaced by civil war in their home country and had journeyed a thousand miles to find refuge. There also were families, particularly women and children, fleeing the war in Sudan.

As the camp grew, young boys were unable to compete for firewood. The solar cookers, developed for the purpose by Warner Merz of Germany, allowed the boys to cook maize and beans in less than four hours and ugali (a mixture of maize, flour and water) in less than two hours, according to TWR archives.

TWR Kenya delivered the solar cookers in partnership with the Lutheran World Federation, Gatere said.

NO PART OF the world was harder hit by HIV/AIDS than sub-Saharan Africa. By 2001, AIDS was the leading cause of death in the region, according to the United Nations' AIDS agency. Of the 40 million people who were living with HIV/AIDS by the end of that year, 28.5 million were in sub-Saharan Africa. Of the 3 million people who died of AIDS worldwide in 2001, 2.2 million were in sub-Saharan Africa.

"It wasn't just an isolated thing," said Tom Watkins, director of Strategic Initiatives & Partnerships for TWR. "It wasn't just like here's somebody dying over here, and there's somebody dying over there. But it was all the

Sudan was also affected by the famine in next-door Ethiopia in 1985, as this photo suggests. Whether famine or AIDS or COVID, TWR Africa has played a role in responding.

orphans. I mean, just unbelievable the fallout from one disease – a whole generation of orphans being created, either that or single-parent families."

In the early 2000s, Watkins was appointed to co-ordinate HIV/AIDS and holistic ministries for TWR under a global strategic plan created by then-President David Tucker. Watkins felt compassion for those affected by HIV/AIDS, but he didn't feel qualified to lead the effort.

Then, he said, the Lord showed him: "That's exactly why I want you to do this, because you're not qualified, and you know I need you to depend on me."

In his research, Watkins connected with Kerus Global Education, a biblically based nonprofit that focuses on public health and education issues, including HIV/AIDS. Kerus had developed "It Takes Courage!" a curriculum that Watkins describes as a character-based abstinence program.

The people at Kerus were excited about the possibility of reaching a larger audience through media, Watkins said. So the TWR team worked with them to develop an audio drama called *Grandma's Village*.

A Kenyan man builds a solar box cooker in this 1995 photo. TWR contributed the cookers to the massive Kakuma Refugee Camp, originally opened in 1992 to house the "lost boys of Sudan."

Talking about abstinence wasn't politically correct with the "intelligentsia," Watkins said. But "nobody else could find a solution that was better than abstinence."

Swaziland (now Eswatini) had the world's highest prevalence of HIV infections in the early 2000s, according to the U.S. Centers for Disease Control and Prevention. In 2006, 64% of all deaths in Swaziland were related to HIV/AIDS, the World Health Organization reported.

TWR and its national partner in the country, Voice of the Church, responded with *The Honey That Kills*, which was created by TWR Kenya, and its own program beginning in 2008, *Leave a Legacy*. Both emphasize abstinence and faithfulness. A call-in program on HIV and AIDS in Swaziland was "groundbreaking," Watkins said, because "these were things people just absolutely did not talk about in that culture."

It's interesting to note that as these programs aired, the rate of new HIV infections in Swaziland decreased by 68% from 2008 to 2020.

In Uganda, which embraced the abstinence-based teachings, mother-to-child HIV infections dropped from 30% in 2000 to 2.8% in 2022, according to the Ministry of Health.

"Uganda was one of the really, really big success stories early on that hardly anybody could refute," Watkins said. "And it made people so mad. The people ... were trying to put down abstinence ... but the data was just overwhelming."

Under Gatere's direction, TWR Kenya "in a lot of ways was our flagship" for HIV/AIDS efforts, Watkins said. "Bernice was really one of our great vision keepers and champions and creative thinkers."

VETERAN TWR MISSIONARY Bill Mial was on a red-eye flight from Raleigh, North Carolina, to London in the early 2000s when he became engaged in conversation with a fellow passenger. She had heard him on a Christian radio broadcast that morning, and their conversation led to his desire to find a doctor who could write scripts on basic health and hygiene issues from a Christian perspective.

The woman woke up her husband, Dr. Ron Halbrooks, who at the time was practicing at Duke University in Durham, North Carolina. Halbrooks was enthused, to say the least. He ended up writing 52 15-minute programs while he and his family were serving at a clinic in East Asia and producing them with TWR Hong Kong.

That was the beginning of the program known as *Dr. Luke*. As of 2023, more than 100 episodes were being aired in eight languages, including African French, Hindi, Swahili and Somali, with additional languages in online versions.

MORE RECENTLY, TWR responded in a variety of ways when the COVID-19 pandemic broke out.

By the end of June 2020 in Africa, TWR had produced 19 radio spots with accurate, meaningful information on the disease. They were being broadcast on 34 outlets in eight languages. English spots were voiced by President Libby; Jon Fugler, chief content officer; Peggy Banks, then director of TWR Women of Hope; and Lonnie Berger, director of Every Man A Warrior.

As COVID-19 forced many people to grapple with issues of life and death, TWR Asia addressed these concerns with a program called *From Despair to Hope*. Developed in Mandarin, the program was translated into other languages, such as Swahili and Somali in Africa.

At the agency's request, TWR partnered with the U.S. Agency for International Development to present programming in Venezuela about how to avoid contracting COVID, Libby said.

The efforts drew many positive responses.

"You asked for input into what the TWR coronavirus program means to us," one African correspondent wrote. "Well, it has changed our lives and our community. Hearing the great program every day in our home [has] made us aware of attitudes and behaviors we need to change and how much God loves us."

SECTION V

The Wave of the Future

OUR WORLD HAS changed so much since 1954. Think of it. In the early 1950s, Mr. Potato Head debuted. As did RCA's first complete electronic color TV system. But a media revolution would occur in the decades to come, and the media landscape radically changed once smaller, faster computers became widely available.

That paved the way for a broad tech explosion. Eventually, new media hit the scene, and the world was watching, listening, connecting in ways it never had. Radio no longer holds a monopoly on the media market. That doesn't mean radio's effectiveness has waned. It just isn't the only means to connect. Trans World Radio adapted, deciding to present itself to the public as TWR, not to diminish radio but to acknowledge that we are constantly innovating and incorporating new tech-nologies. The emphasis shifted and expanded. We echoed the apostle Paul's words: "I have become all things to all people, so that I may by all means save some" (1 Corinthians 9:22).

Adding new media didn't dilute the message. Instead, it bred creativity. Ideas exploded. And people who had never heard or seen the name of Jesus were starting to ask questions. What will media look like in the future? We don't know but we have some ideas.

"Praise the Lord! I will give thanks to the Lord with all my heart, in the company of the upright and in the assembly. Great are the works of the Lord; they are studied by all who delight in them. Splendid and majestic is His work, and His righteousness endures forever."

— PSALM 111:1-3

21

The Gift of Genuine Friendship

N O MATTER THE hour when adversity strikes, you discover who your true friends are. They promptly rally around you and come alongside to assist in any and every way they can.

TWR experienced that type of close-knit bond in 2017 when an early morning fire broke out in its Cary, North Carolina office – three days before Christmas.

Praise God no one was hurt. But one significant section of the three-story building, nestled in a picturesque, wooded area on the city's edge, was rendered unusable by the fire. Smoke damage was extensive. Fortunately, the speedy response by the Cary Fire Department's Engine 3 and Ladder 3 companies prevented flames from engulfing the entire brick office. While TWR's fire insurance covered a major part of the costs, repair needs were still substantial.

Work was altered. Staff members had to relocate, setting up shop in temporary cubicles in TWR's mostly undamaged dining room and auditorium. But their mission to speak the hope of Jesus Christ to the world pressed ahead with little disruption. The Cary team didn't miss a beat.

Throughout the lengthy renovation phase, TWR supporters showed their love for the ministry. Moved by the Spirit of God and out of an abiding appreciation for its global gospel proclamation, longtime and new donors alike reached out to make the restoration of the building possible. A special rededication ceremony was held Oct. 11, 2018 – 27 years after the Cary office's initial dedication.

"We're extremely thankful to God for everyone's response," TWR's President Lauren Libby said at the time. "People and organizations gave sacrificially. We were blown away by people's generosity to help another ministry in need, which was us. It was the body of Christ coming together. We're eternally indebted to those who had a part in restoring this."

Many of those contributions came from Christian radio stations and their listeners throughout the U.S. Typically, their donations are directed toward a particular TWR overseas project or program or in support of a TWR missionary. Not this time, though.

"Following the Cary fire, the kindness shown to us by these stations and their listeners was inspiring in a different way," said John Summerville, who directs TWR's radio station partnerships. "It went much deeper."

Their commitment transitioned from lending assistance toward TWR's vital kingdom work in distant and remote lands – important and vital as that is – to coming to the aid of a ministry they love and respect in its moment of crisis.

"They showed Christlike qualities of a true friend," Summerville explained. "That's why we refer to these stations and their listeners as our radio friends. What was amazing was how they connected this recovery effort, in their backyard, so to speak, to our overall mission internationally. And they exhibited compassion. That sensitivity touched our hearts."

One of the network responses came from Northwestern Radio in Minnesota. "As soon as we heard of the fire, all of us at Northwestern Media wanted to do something to help," said Scott A. Jones, assistant vice president of business operations and technology for Northwestern Media. "It is such a hard thing to be displaced so unexpectedly, and our only thought was to love on our brothers and sisters at TWR.

"They all do such amazing work," he added, "and it's an honor to be a part of their story."

THE ORIGIN OF many of these friendships can be traced back to the dawning of the new millennium. That's when TWR began ramping up its radio partnerships. TWR leadership extended invitations to Christian radio executives and other key personnel to visit ongoing ministries in the field.

Their goal? To enable these broadcasters to witness firsthand what God was doing in the lives of people as they listened to evangelistic and Bible-teaching programs over TWR in their heart language; similar programs aired over their own station but in English. Upon their return, they explored how they could enhance TWR's ministry by engaging their listeners in specific campaigns and eliciting their volunteer financial participation in TWR's global outreach.

The TWR office in Cary, North Carolina, was extensively damaged in a fire on Dec. 22, 2017. TWR's radio partners in the U.S. quickly responded to help meet the need. TWR's Sterling Ottun was among those who helped with cleanup after the 2017 fire.

The first trip was in 2003 to South Africa, Mozambique, Malawi and Swaziland (now known as Eswatini), followed a year later by visiting TWR's work in Brazil, Uruguay and Bolivia.

For that initial trip, TWR approached several well-known radio networks, including Northwestern Media, which is affiliated with Northwestern College (now University of Northwestern-St. Paul). Paul Ramseyer was then serving as its vice president, and he tapped Paul Harkness to go. He was at that time station manager of Life 97.3/Faith 90.5 in Duluth, Minnesota, and was serving on the missions funding team for the Northwestern Radio Network.

Harkness had been to Kenya in 2001 to install studios at Daystar University's Athi River campus. "That was my first trip to Africa, and I fell in love with the people, culture, students and staff," he said. "So when the invitation came to travel with TWR, I jumped at the opportunity to return."

While Harkness was impressed with the dedication of the staff and the impact of Christian broadcasts in each country, Malawi's "kind and gentle people" especially captured his heart.

Marching on Palm Sunday through a village with 1,300 Malawians waving palm branches and hearing them praise Jesus in the Chichewa language proved to be a memorable highlight. On that same trip, Harkness was fascinated by a radio rally held under a thorn bush tree at the crossroads of two dirt roads by a school. The radio station staff set up a keyboard and amplifier and started singing as people gathered. School children and Christian radio leaders joined in and, before long, the crowd was praising the Lord and expressing their joy through exuberant traditional African dancing.

The importance of Christian radio in Malawi was not lost on prominent government leaders. "I heard from TWR staff that government representatives from another part of Malawi had heard about TWR stations and were insisting that their part of the country get TWR there, too," Harkness noted.

As the trip wound down, he came away yearning to help the station's staff, who were operating their station with limited funds and aging equipment yet were committed to serving the region with the gospel of Christ through radio.

Upon his return, he solicited the help of colleagues Neil Stavem and Dan Wynia, and the trio pitched to the missions funding team the idea of raising money for equipment so the Malawi staff could establish a network of FM stations in multiple cities across Malawi. The team loved the idea and approved it for the network's share-a-thon later that fall. Their listeners enthusiastically embraced the project and gladly contributed.

Since that trip in 2003, Northwestern Media – buoyed by its faithful listeners – has continued contributing toward multiple TWR projects around the world. These have focused on meeting needs not only on the African continent but also on the Pacific island of Guam and on the Caribbean island of Bonaire, as well in Singapore and in the region served by the Pakistan, Afghanistan and North India (PANI) transmitter.

And, of course, the needs arising in Cary, North Carolina, after the 2017 fire.

ALSO ON THAT trip to Africa was Leighton LeBoeuf, who was serving as general manager of WMBW in Chattanooga, part of the Moody Radio Network. At the time, LeBoeuf had no idea how that trip would also have major career ramifications for one of his longtime morning hosts.

Tugging at LeBoeuf's heart was a studio and transmitter upgrade project in Mozambique. WMBW's listeners rallied around this project, and the goal was met.

Andy Napier, who had been at the station for about 15 years, helped on-air with that campaign. That was his first exposure to TWR, and he liked what he heard. Over the ensuing years when various TWR staff traveled through Chattanooga, Napier requested that they stop by WMBW for interviews. Listeners received on-air updates about how the Lord was using TWR to accomplish Christ's Great Commission to make disciples of all nations. Napier helped with various follow-up campaigns.

"I was seeing God at work around the world, and as a result, the Lord was working in my life, giving me a heart not just for local missions but also for global missions," Napier said.

One morning, Napier had an eye-opening conversation with his wife, Kathy. Though completely content professionally, he wondered what his long-term job goals might look like. Kathy stunned him with her reply. "Well, why don't you go on Trans World Radio's website and see what might be there."

Napier did just that and discovered one missionary posting for someone who could create a radio program highlighting what God was doing through TWR. He gasped. Of his own volition, Napier had already been doing something very much like this as part of his WMBW duties. So, he immediately contacted John Summerville and talked about that position.

Andy and Kathy prayed about this possible move and, though they had deep Chattanooga family roots, they obeyed God's calling. The Lord provided their missionary support, and they moved to Cary in 2013.

Today, Andy produces *Footsteps*, a daily two-minute feature heard on more than 220 radio outlets across the U.S. And he has had the privilege of traveling overseas to such places as Austria, Ecuador, Slovakia, Portugal, Malawi and South Africa.

One trip stands out. It was to distribute radios to students at the Ekwendeni School for the Visually Impaired in northern Malawi. About 50 middle-school- and high-school-aged children live on campus.

The students grinned ear-to-ear, and their ecstatic shouts of glee echoed through the area when they received the radios. Napier's heart leapt for joy. But one particular phrase during a *Footsteps* interview with the school's administrator arrested his attention.

"We are making a fellowship together in the name of the Lord," the Rev. Timothy Nyirenda told Napier.

That statement was like a bolt of lightning, penetrating Napier's thinking. "To be honest, up until that point, when I thought of church fellowship, images of potluck suppers on a Wednesday night or getting together at someone's home during the week came to mind," he said. "But there in the middle of Malawi, an African reverend opened my eyes to the fact that true Christian fellowship is when we lock arms with each other, and we partner to accomplish Great Commission ministry work together."

That refreshing image continues to fuel Napier's passion to team with other believers to reach every last people group remaining on earth with the gospel.

HAVING A GROWING love for those who still need to hear about Jesus also characterizes the team at Montrose Broadcasting in Pennsylvania and New York. They had an "inside" perspective on TWR since one of the global media ministry's founding directors, Arnie Robertson, was married to one of Montrose Broadcasting's former staff members, and the couple lived in Montrose.

"It was only logical for us to partner with Trans World Radio," Larry Souder said. Larry was president of the broadcast corporation in 2004 when he and his wife, Patti, traveled to South America with the TWR group. "We were glad to go, and Arnie was quite pleased that we were doing it."

Larry and Patti enjoyed exploring TWR's work in Brazil, Paraguay and Bolivia but chose to focus on Bolivia. The staff and facilities at its flagship station impressed them with their excellence in providing gospel programming in Spanish, Quechua and Low German.

Two teen girls amazed them by hosting a regularly scheduled radio program for young people. Larry and Patti witnessed its impact as they watched dozens of people gather for a Father's Day celebration planned by the girls.

On Sunday, they attended an open-air sunday school and church service where they were touched by the enthusiastic singing and preaching. Later that day, they participated in a radio rally at which hundreds of people expressed their gratitude and enthusiasm for Christian radio.

One of the highlights they'll never forget was a visit to a Quechua village, where they were warmly welcomed. Through translators, village leaders told of their intense longing to have Christian radio in their language. They were deeply concerned about their young people because secular radio was gaining in popularity.

"Seeing the enthusiasm in the radio rallies and in the Quechua village reminded me of similar excitement for Christian radio that we experienced in the early days of our radio stations," Patti said. "WPEL came on the air in 1953, and sister station WPGM came to Danville in 1964. To hear people in Bolivia tell us of their deep-seated desire for similar biblical programming and music in their towns and villages brought tears to my eyes. We knew our listeners would relate to that."

And indeed, they did! Larry and Patti went back home fired up about going to their listeners with the need to raise funds for equipment for a Christian radio station in San Julian, then the 31st-most-populated city in the country, according to census figures. That need was met, and a team of three engineers traveled to Bolivia and helped the staff there install it.

"The talented personnel there knew what programming was needed to reach out and minister to their community," Larry explained. "What we did was provide the equipment so they could accomplish it. We didn't at all try to tell them how to run their station. And that helped foster a closer relationship between us and them."

That led four years later to a second equipment project for a station in Trinidad, the 12th-largest city in Bolivia. Once again, the same three engineers helped with the installation, locking arms with their Bolivian compatriots.

In 2017, the partnership focus shifted toward helping TWR's global Women of Hope ministry, which includes radio programming that can be heard in 70-plus languages. At the same time, Montrose Broadcasting redirected its attention to assisting TWR in Malawi.

When the leadership baton was passed to James Baker in 2017, he sensed the Lord's leading to expand to Africa. For one recent project, contributions from Montrose listeners far exceeded their goal, enabling TWR to refurbish not only the control room at a station in Malawi's capital city of Lilongwe but also its studio. That facility now serves as the flagship operation for an FM network crisscrossing the country. And Montrose has also been able to raise funds necessary to replace aging equipment in many of the transmitters in that network of stations.

The Lilongwe station is a constant beehive of activity. "Local pastors from around Malawi come and record programming in that studio," Baker said. "It's also being used by teenagers and college-age students, whose programs are targeting Malawi's youth."

Baker is thrilled that Montrose listeners are helping Malawi Christians to make an impact in the lives of millions of people. "Talk about paying eternal dividends when you're doing a project!" he said.

James and his wife, Chris, had the honor of traveling to the East African country to see the fruit of their collaboration with TWR. They joined Ken Cummins, general manager of Missionary Radio WNKJ of Hopkinsville, Kentucky. Together, along with TWR staff, they handed out two sets of 50 solar-powered radios, toward which WNKJ listeners donated funds.

Ken and his wife, Tammy, had been introduced to TWR when they visited its AM station on Bonaire. Afterward, WNKJ participated in TWR's Power Up campaign to boost the transmitting power from the island so more people throughout Latin America could hear the station – and thereby the good news of Jesus Christ. Missionary Radio listeners have been faithful supporters of multiple TWR projects, and TWR staff, including Summerville and Napier, have relished making the 602-mile trek to Kentucky to take part in WNKJ's two yearly fundraisers (Care-a-thon and Friendraiser).

So anticipation was building to see what God would reveal to everyone in Malawi. They weren't disappointed.

As soon as the TWR vehicle arrived at the special gatherings, dozens of smiling children surrounded their guests. James quickly took photos of Chris surrounded by 20 to 30 children wanting to make her feel welcome.

"These were joyous occasions, filled with heartfelt singing," Baker said. "The people were so happy we were there and that we cared enough about them."

JOHN OWENS, GOING on nine years as general manager of The Light FM, based in Asheville, North Carolina, has sensed that same spirit of thankfulness in his travels with TWR.

The Light FM is a regional group of nine FM stations operated by Blue Ridge Broadcasting and a listener-supported ministry of the Billy Graham Evangelistic Association.

Owens first heard about TWR when he was working at WMHK in Columbia, South Carolina. His initial trip with John Summerville was to Lithuania.

The Light FM had a prior partnership with TWR before Owens arrived. BGEA's Jim Kirkland joined Summerville in traveling to Estonia and Ukraine in 2010. Station listeners generously donated funds toward equipment upgrades in Estonia, providing a stronger AM signal that could be picked up as far away as Moscow and Ukraine, as well as in Estonia, Latvia, Lithuania and Belarus.

"Partnering with TWR is something we love," Owens said. "God has provided us with a similar calling to reach people with the gospel using audio and radio. We're always ready for another opportunity to work with them!"

Through Owens' travels to West Africa during the past several years, The Light FM has established a strong connection with a sister station in the region, known as WATS, whose location can't be publicly identified for security reasons. That station produces and airs programs throughout West Africa via one powerful transmitter and specifically targets Nigeria over another transmitter.

The general manager's enthusiasm for and commitment to the power of radio partnerships bubbles over when he talks about a unique alliance between TWR and Compassion International that took place in northern Ghana in late 2023. John and his wife, Tamara, have sponsored four children through Compassion, including a 21-year-old young man who has graduated from the University of Ghana.

"I pitched an idea to TWR and Compassion International on collaborating to provide windup radios with attached flashlights to the families of the kids in the Compassion program," he explained. "These radios would enable the families to hear solid, biblically based programming from the station in West Africa. At the same time, Compassion could work through local churches to not only help disciple these children but also to reach their extended families with the gospel of Jesus Christ."

Both organizations ministered side by side in October 2023, and Owens and TWR staff traveled to two Compassion projects to distribute 50 radios at each.

Owens set the scene. "Now, picture this. It's night. It's a remote area of Ghana. And it's pitch-black outside. So when the kids and their families turned on the flashlights, they went crazy!"

It was like a symphony of fireflies dancing in the air.

"These are two high-integrity ministries teaming together for the glory of God," he said. "It was a success. I thank God for all that he did through the idea he gave us and the partnership that was created."

Children in northern Ghana look on as windup radios and attached flashlights were distributed in late 2023. The event grew out of a partnership between John Owens of The Light FM, Compassion International and TWR. Photo used with permission from Compassion International.

*"I will cause Your Name to be remembered
in all generations; therefore the peoples
will give You thanks forever and ever."*

— PSALM 45:17

22

Living Water to New Generations

IT WAS ON the Atlas Road in Morocco that Ralf Stores had an epiphany.

"You could go miles and miles and miles and not get drinking water," Stores said of the seven-day journey in the late 1990s. "But you could find a Coke."

It triggered a thought about the purpose of the Church, recalled Stores, the director of media services for TWR.

"If Coca-Cola can be ... so focused on getting a Coke into every place in the world, why can't we bring them living water and the saving knowledge of Jesus?" he asked.

Now for seven-plus decades, TWR has been bringing the saving knowledge of Jesus to the world through mass media. For much of its history, that meant radio. It has come to mean more, including TWR360, the internet ministry that Stores leads.

A typical road sign in Morocco. "You could go miles and miles and miles and not get drinking water," Ralf Stores said. "But you could find a Coke."

TWR360, TODAY ENCOMPASSING hundreds of ministries in more than 140 languages, goes back only as far as 2012.

It started as Stores considered the changing media landscape. "While radio still is one of the most predominant forms there is of getting the gospel out, we still had to explore these other opportunities," Stores said.

Stores realized there were Bible-based programs available in a variety of languages online, but they came through English-based websites. People who didn't know English as a second language wouldn't be able to find the programs in their preferred languages.

"So the vision was to develop a website where somebody could come and engage and get content in their heart language anytime, anywhere, on any connected device without having to go through an English portal," Stores said.

Thus, TWR360 loads on the computer in the same language that the individual's browser uses. If that's Arabic, TWR360 opens in Arabic. The individual doesn't have to search for Arabic on the site.

TWR360 was launched in May 2013 with five languages and a handful of ministries.

The multitude of options available now ranges from blogs to worship services to videos to Scripture readings. Whether already a believer or curious about Christianity, the guest on the website can watch the *JESUS* film, listen to worship music, listen to a passage from the Daily Audio Bible or embark on the in-depth study of the Word in a *Thru the Bible* program, among many other choices. If she has a specific interest, she can find teachings grouped under any of 60 topics, from "Addictions & Recovery" to "Science & the Bible" to "Who Is God?" – in her heart language.

In this Nepalese man's homeland, the predominant religion is Hinduism. But whether in Nepal or in the U.S., Nepalese can hear about Jesus in their own language via TWR360.

Those who come to TWR programs via the internet are appreciative. This earnest plea came from Benin in response to French programming: "Help me to know the Lord Jesus Christ even more. I want to live a life with Christ, but my flesh is very much used to the pleasures of the world. Support me. I want to come to Christ and have a new life."

It is significant that TWR360 is popular in hard-to-reach places. "Some of the people who access TWR360 do so at a great cost to themselves because when they visit a foreign website it is a trackable event.

More TWR360 page views come from India than from any other country. Other countries with high numbers of views include Ukraine, Brazil, the United States and Indonesia. During the height of the COVID-19 pandemic, someone from India offered this joyful response to English-language programming: "In spite of so much sickness and fear, God has drawn our attention to the greatest hope we have in the good news of Jesus Christ! More people are listening to the amazing work of Christ on the cross. The church in India will never be the same! Our Lord God is turning this pandemic into a season of hope. God bless every person in TWR, and may he alone be glorified!"

IT'S NEW MEDIA, but Stores said two of its greatest advocates are two of TWR's longest-serving missionaries, Jim Hill (39 years with TWR in 2023) and Tom Streeter (51 years).

Streeter, who is such a fan that his North Carolina license plate reads "TWR360," sees it as an effective ministry resource for use in North America as well as the rest of the world. He notes that in 2020, more than 20% of U.S. residents told the Census Bureau they speak a language other than English in their homes. With TWR360, their Christian neighbors and co-workers have a resource they can share in the heart languages of the foreigners in their midst.

Streeter always has with him a packet of business-type cards in a variety of TWR360 languages that point recipients to the website, and he prays regularly that he'll encounter someone whose language matches one of his cards.

Once, in a nearby Walmart, Streeter struck up a conversation with an employee who inquired about TWR. Because the employee had a noticeable accent, Streeter asked him what his heart language was.

"He said, 'Well, I'm from Nepal.' And I didn't say it out loud, but to myself and the Lord, I said, 'YES!' Because I knew that I had put a Nepali card in my packet of cards."

By the time he left the store, Streeter had given the man a Nepali 360 card.

TWR360 provides an excellent tool North American Christians can use to point their foreign neighbors and co-workers to Christ, Streeter said. "To me, the internet is the most exciting expansion of ministry that I've seen in TWR's world of ministry, primarily because it opens up the opportunity to share the gospel with the immigrant community here in the U.S. as well as the rest of the world."

"He put a new song in my mouth,

a song of praise to our God;

many will see and fear,

and will trust in the Lord."

— PSALM 40:3

23

Sharing the Story via Video

A ICHA* THOUGHT IT was a joke when someone suggested she approach TWR to create videos for her ministry in North Africa.

"Oh, you mean the radio ministry?" Aicha said, laughing as she related the story in a 2022 talk to TWR's European National Partners Conference.

She and her team of church planters felt called by God to use video and social media to connect with a certain people group, the majority of whom come from a Muslim background. They needed videos that felt local and were in the heart language of the people.

The opportunity was there, but Aicha's team lacked video expertise, so they searched for a video producer to help them.

It was 2014 when she reached out to TWR and met Tyler Gates, the director of TWR's new video team.

* Not her real name for security reasons

Gates, who previously led a video production company in Alaska, had been called to TWR in 2012 as the mission's full-time video specialist. Gates was passionate about sharing the gospel through video. By then, smartphones were ubiquitous. YouTube, launched in 2005, had become so influential internationally that it was credited with a major role in the "Arab Spring" anti-government protests in 2011.

"YouTube is reaching people and people groups and segments of the population that missionaries dream of reaching," Gates said in an interview. "But when they go on there to search for cat videos or the latest football scores or something like that, are they going to see the gospel?"

The project Aicha envisioned aligned with Gates' passion to use video to share the gospel. The goal was to create a series of videos that told the stories of the Bible, starting with creation and ending with the resurrection of Jesus.

Aicha and Gates decided animation would be the best approach. And Gates already had a digital illustrator in mind – Kayla Schlipf, a former TWR intern. In 2016, she agreed and began what would become a two-year project. It was also in 2016 that Gates coined the name MOTION for the new TWR ministry.

"TWR MOTION has brought to life visually and contextually the Bible in ways that are very digestible because the nice thing about doing animation is that it is language agnostic," Gates said.

Share the Story, a 20-episode series of Bible stories, was the project that launched MOTION as a ministry of TWR. This project helped the team see the need church planters have for videos in their disciple-making efforts.

In 2017, amid the project, Gates was called to a different work. Candace Mackie, a MOTION team member since 2014, took over as director.

The Lord shaped her vision for the ministry through a course called Foundations of Media Strategy, Mackie said. In the course, which she took in 2017, she learned how church planters are using marketing on social media to identify people who are spiritually open and to start conversations with them. The catalyst for those conversations is often videos.

"I just started to really understand how our content was going to be used, which made me want to bend over backwards to help [the North

Africa] team even more than just developing the animations," Mackie said. "Like, how can we supply you guys with ads? How can we get graphics to you that you can use on your social media pages? What do you need? Let us help you with the bigger campaign, not just the videos."

That's what she did. In addition to developing the animated Bible stories, the MOTION team developed ads and other resources for their three-month campaign, which launched in January 2018.

"[The content produced by MOTION] was palatable for our people group," Aicha said. "Their dedication to biblical accuracy as well as contextualization continued to encourage our small team on the field, and we created something really beautiful."

It was incredible to see how God used the series to transform lives. About 1,200 people connected with the church-planting team online. Ninety-nine people met with a local believer in person to study the Bible. And seven people were baptized during that period.

In early 2023, the TWR MOTION team traveled to Thailand for research purposes after a church-planting team there requested them to develop a new animation series, *Journey to Hope*, geared toward Buddhists. Andrew Haas (from left), Candace Mackie, Kayla Schlipf, Hannah McGurk, Mary Vooys and Rachel Mehlhaff pause during their explorations. Vooys is a contract illustrator working with MOTION on this project.

Senior illustrator and animator Kayla Schlipf has been part of the TWR MOTION team since 2015.

Many viewers wrestled over what they watched; it challenged their worldview.

One viewer wrote, "I am waiting for your episode tonight. I am hoping to see the truth. Right now, I am afraid of God, and I can't control these feelings. I am very afraid that I am on the wrong path. My problem isn't in knowing the stories of the prophets [who lived] before the prophet Jesus – not at all. I know them well. And I believe them.

"My issue is what I should believe now. Should I be a Christian and believe in the crucifixion and be persuaded completely to be a Christian?

"Or should I be a Muslim and be fully persuaded before it's too late?

"Before me are two paths; which one is true?"

IN 2022, MOTION released a second video series called *He Changed Me*, which presents testimonies of Muslim-background believers. Because of the power of social media and video in identifying people already on a spiritual journey, more church planters are adopting this approach. As of early 2024, *Share the Story* and *He Changed Me* were available in 27 languages between them and being used by church-planting teams in about 40 countries. The exact number of teams is unknown, but MOTION partners with 26 organizations to make these videos available to church-planting teams around the world.

TWR MOTION animations are carefully designed to tell the story of the gospel in a culturally relatable way. This crucifixion scene is from *Share the Story*, created with Muslims in mind.

That's why MOTION continues to produce new animated series. The seven-person team creates videos that help people all over the world imagine what it would look like to follow Jesus in their contexts – no matter their religious or cultural background.

But it's not just about one person coming to faith. TWR MOTION's vision is built on the team's desire to make disciples. Their desire is that the videos would play a role in groups of people coming to faith that would multiply into more and more groups.

So far, MOTION has never looked for work, Mackie said. Church planters have come to them.

And that's the team's mission: to make videos that church planters can use online as part of their digital strategy to find and make disciples.

In 2023, at the request of a church-planting team in Thailand, the team began production of a new animation series geared toward Buddhists. MOTION's work for church planters is a good example of why partnership is a key concept for TWR.

"The apostle Paul talked about it," Libby said. "He said: 'I planted, Apollos watered, but God gave the increase.' And so it's the idea of partnering together to bring the gospel to the whole world."

"Thy word is a lamp to my feet,

and a light to my path."

— PSALM 119:105

24

Telling the Story in a Fresh Way

THE PEOPLE OF TWR are always looking for new and fresh ways to proclaim the unchangeable truth of the Word of God.

Even as this book was in process, TWR was moving quickly toward making a solid discipleship tool available to a much larger audience.

Brazilian Bible scholar Luiz Sayão created an audio Bible commentary designed to resonate with people whose worldview is framed by a secular mindset.

Sayão began developing the 613-episode program in 2006 in cooperation with TWR partner Radio Trans Mundial* Brazil. He named it *Route 66* or, in Portuguese, *Rota 66*. The title marries the 66 books of the Bible with the famous U.S. Route 66. It has been renamed *Mission 66* for its wider TWR distribution.

"*Route 66* is explaining the Bible, but in a practical way that the person will understand, believe in Jesus [and start] serving the Lord," Sayão said. "So we hope that we can together do the only homework that our

Lord gave to us: 'You go and tell this to all the nations.'"

A down-to-earth intellectual, Sayão spent three years assembling all the 30-minute episodes. He took care to make his teaching both accurate and relatable.

"Luiz is very kind with the listener," said Esteban Larrosa, TWR vice president for Latin America, the Caribbean and U.S. Hispanic ministries. "He speaks with the heart of a pastor who's trying to communicate with passion and emotion what he believes."

Sayão, who traveled to the U.S. office of TWR in Cary, North Carolina, in March 2023 to finalize and sign the agreement to widen distribution of the program, said he strives to connect the culture to the biblical content. For example, when speaking of the creation, he refers to the rendition by jazz great Louis Armstrong of "What a Wonderful World."

Sayão also includes humor in his teaching. "It's not a comedy," he said. "But there are some things there, like when you read Proverbs, you see the lazy guy. He says, 'No, no, I don't go outside. There is a lion out there.' It's a little bit funny."

Sayão came to this work with impeccable credentials and a compelling life story. His childhood was so traumatic that at age 10 he contemplated taking his own life. But at 12, influenced by a cousin, he surrendered his life to Christ and was baptized. At 13, he committed his life to the Lord's service.

He earned advanced degrees at the University of São Paulo and the Baptist Theological College of São Paulo, where he taught before becoming a professor at Pioneer Baptist College. Able to speak seven languages fluently, he led a team of scholars translating the New International Version of the Bible into Portuguese.

Since 2009, Sayão has been leading tours of Bible lands, and he has been to Israel almost 60 times. It was on one of those trips that he met the leader of a Chinese group. She was a Christian, he learned, but was not allowed to mention that to her group. She was able to attend his presentation one night but had to leave before it was over. They met each other again at breakfast on the last day of his tour.

"She said, 'Oh, professor, it's you,'" he recounted. "'I'm sorry, I can-

Luiz Sayão (front left) and his colleague Jonatas Hubner tape an interview with TWR's Andy Napier (back right) and John Lundy. Sayão and Hubner were in Cary, North Carolina, in March 2023 to finalize an agreement to broaden distribution of their program.

not spend much time away from my group. But we need so much of biblical teaching in China. ... Can you help us somehow?'"

That's why Mandarin, the primary language of China, became the first language into which *Mission 66* was translated from Portuguese. It has been aired in China since October 2020.

"The *Mission 66* program was very helpful to me," a listener in Beijing wrote. "The content healed my depression and helped me find meaning and value in life."

The program also is heard in Africa, in Portuguese-speaking Mozambique, where it has been broadcast on partner station Radio Capital since March 2021.

"How I have listened to *Mission 66* with keen interest as it helped me

Sayão speaks at the TWR U.S. office in Cary, North Carolina, about the 613-episode *Rota 66* he developed in cooperation with Radio Trans Mundial Brazil. TWR seeks to make it available in the world's 10 most-spoken languages as *Mission 66*.

to follow the biblical narrative," one African listener wrote. "It is our Bible guide. I like the discussion of practical examples, such as issues of handling personal conflicts."

"We're committed to a biblical overview for people, particularly globally, in some areas of the world [where] there is no opportunity to have that," Libby said.

The first phase of expanding the program will be to bring *Mission 66* to the world's 10 major languages, Larrosa said. That began in 2023 with audio translations in production in Spanish, English and Japanese, and the way being prepared for several others.

Sayão said he was excited to share the truth of Scripture and therefore to find "new brothers and sisters all over the world."

"The Bible is alive," he said. "Even for me today, I can read the Bible in Hebrew, in Greek. ... Every time I find out things that I hadn't seen before. It's amazing, the power of the Bible."

* *Radio Trans Mundial is the Portuguese and Spanish equivalent of Trans World Radio.*

"I will give thanks to You, O Lord, among the peoples, and I will sing praises to You among the nations. For Your lovingkindness is great above the heavens, and Your truth reaches to the skies."

— PSALM 108:3-4

25

The Unreached Are Not Forgotten

HOW DO YOU reach a foot soldier of ISIS? Start with his grandmother, with whom the young man kept strong family ties. A grandmother who was a faithful listener of TWR programs.

"I was a member of ISIS," said Hafeez.* "When ISIS began to dissolve and the army started to take control, I got scared and escaped."

But where could he go and feel safe? He fled to his grandmother's house.

"While I was hiding, I began to question my Muslim faith."

That's when Hafeez's grandmother shared a story from her own past. Thirty to 40 years prior, she was fiddling with her radio when she discovered a station that talked about Jesus. It was TWR's powerful station in Monte Carlo. First she was intrigued, then she was hooked. The more she listened, the more she learned, and the more she was drawn to Jesus. She came to the point that

* Not his real name to protect his privacy

she could no longer keep from entrusting her life to him. And that's what she did. She received him as Savior and kept following him as Lord.

"She said to me, 'I haven't ever told anyone this. Will you become a believer, too?'" Hafeez said. "I prayed with my grandmother that day and put my faith in Jesus."

Hafeez then took a bold step. He came out of hiding and decided to be baptized at a conference in the Middle East. It was being held to train Muslim-background believers through the *Discipleship Essentials* materials developed by TWR Canada.

Today, Hafeez is learning how to nurture others in their Christian faith. He's putting into practice the truth of 2 Timothy 2:2 – "The things which you have heard from me in the presence of many witnesses, entrust these to faithful men who will be able to teach others also)."

WHAT BEGAN IN 1954 as a ministry to reach Spain with the gospel has grown into a worldwide missionary media enterprise in more than 200 languages with listeners in 190-plus countries. But TWR's core commitment has remained rock solid: proclaiming the good news of Jesus Christ by mass media to men, women, boys and girls wherever they may live.

People like Divsimar,* whose home is in Nepal. Though he read a slew of religious books, he remained skeptical. One day, he opened a Bible.

"An inner voice told me that Jesus is really God, and complete peace came into my heart," he recalled.

However, Divsimar had no one to guide him in his newfound faith journey. Until he was introduced to the radio program *Heralds of Hope* broadcast by TWR.

"My joy knew no bounds," he said. "The program helped me understand the Word of God better and fed me nutrients as a baby Christian."

Today, Divsimar's family worships the Lord!

ALL THESE YEARS since that inaugural broadcast, TWR's leadership and staff keep looking for new and effective ways to reach still more!

"TWR exists for the Great Commission," said Jon Fugler, who came to TWR in 2018 from a longtime background in U.S. Christian radio. He serves as chief content officer. "TWR is helping to reach the world. When I joined on, I boarded a plane that was already flying. To be able to take my skills and my passions in media and do kingdom work like this is a great privilege."

Identifying and targeting unreached people groups is of utmost importance. "We build our content and on-the-ground ministry around that," Fugler said. "It's a unanimous consensus among our leadership, and we've renewed that commitment every year. It's a must-do high priority."

TWR President Lauren Libby concurs. "One of the things we do annually is to affirm the primacy of proclaiming the gospel to unreached people groups, no matter where they are in the world," he said. "Beginning with Dr. Freed, our founder, TWR has had a heart for the unreached peoples of the world. We're constantly asking how can get in there to broadcast or to reach them on their cellphones."

Every spring, TWR recognizes the International Day for the Unreached, calling attention to the 1 in 3 people on the planet who have never heard of Jesus. It was established by the Alliance for the Unreached, a movement that Fugler founded in 2015 when he was serving with Reach Beyond (formerly HCJB). Its campaign goes by the name "A Third of Us."

A Nepalese man proudly displays his radio. In Nepal, 218 of the 227 people groups haven't yet been reached for Christ, according to Joshua Project. Reaching such groups is part of TWR's DNA.

TWR's purpose remains singular: focusing on the world's least-reached people groups and how to "bring them out of darkness and the shadow of death, and burst their bonds apart" (Psalm 104:17).

"Media is an excellent way of introducing the gospel into an unreached people group," Libby noted.

That's certainly true within the Muslim world, which garners a great deal of attention among TWR leader-ship. "We are investing a lot of resources into this," Fugler said.

One program that is making a lasting spiritual difference is *The Way of Righteousness.* It's produced in partnership with ROCK International and has been acclaimed for its effectiveness at explaining the truth of the gospel within the cultural context of Muslims seeking to understanding the Bible. Originally created by missionary Paul Bramsen for the Wolof people of Senegal in West Africa, the program now airs in nearly 40 languages in several African, Central Asian and Middle Eastern countries.

Villagers gather at a meeting place in Suriname. Having come to faith in Christ since the 1960s, the Wayana and Trio tribes now seek to use radio to share the good news with nearby tribes.

The Way of Righteousness is a series of 100 programs that start in Genesis and go through the Book of Acts. The first 50 programs cover the Old Testament and concentrate on the patriarchs, the prophets and the prophecies surrounding the coming of Christ. The next 50 center around the life and ministry of Christ and then the establishment of the early church following his death and resurrection.

Nathan Anderson, TWR's director of ministry in North Africa, is tasked with developing the media ministry's outreach to Kurdish people in places like Syria, southern Türkiye and northern Iraq. There and in countries like Morocco and Algeria, he is working to bring revitalized productions of programs such as *The Way of Righteousness, Women of Hope* and *Power in Persecution*. Through a partner ministry in Türkiye, TWR is strategically collaborating with a Christian radio station in the southern part of the country where there is a large population of Kurds.

One listener wrote to TWR about how *The Way of Righteousness* has ministered to him. "I was Muslim, and I gave my life to Jesus Christ, but my parents persecute me and do everything to me to deny Christ. I had regressed, but after listening to your program *The Way of Righteousness*, I decided to follow Christ again. I know that I will be a victim of oppression, contempt and persecution. I need your support in prayer to go ahead in my walk with the Lord Jesus Christ."

Anderson noted, "I think *The Way of Righteousness* is moving us in the right direction of how to produce good content for Muslim audiences."

·||||·

ON A TOTALLY different continent half a world away, the Wayana and Trio tribes were at one time unreached. After several years of Bible, medical and dental training, Ivan and Doris Schoen – and their three children – packed up their belongings and, under God's leading, headed to the dense interior jungles of Suriname north of Brazil. Beginning in the 1960s, they pioneered literacy work and Bible translation. Today, 80% to 90% of the Wayana and Trio are literate and considered evangelized, with a thriving vibrant church among them.

The couple's son Tom has joined TWR's missionary family and is leading a radio station project among the Wayana and Trio people, who are witnessing to other tribes with similar languages in Brazil, Guyana and

French Guiana. Among them are the "Naked Ones," a Brazilian tribe given that nickname by the Trio and Wayana evangelists.

A longtime pastor and fluent in three Suriname languages, Tom is serving as the on-the-ground liaison between the Suriname government and the tribal leaders for licensing and subsequent implementation. He is working with a Suriname team to build two radio transmission stations and train indigenous people to maintain and operate them. He's also training people to produce broadcast-ready material.

More and more younger Wayana and Trio people are fanning out deeper into the jungle, and church elders fear they are losing touch with the next generation. They are leaving either in search of new sources of food and fertile land for planting or looking for work in the timber, gold, oil or bauxite industries to provide basic necessities for their families. The older leaders believe radio is central to helping to reach the lost and disciple new believers, not only among their own people, but also among those other tribes.

"The Wayana and Trio have expressed on numerous occasions their excitement about the radio ministry, not only for themselves but because it represents a wonderful tool for them to take the gospel to these unreached people groups," Tom said.

Libby noted, "Here's a tribe that was almost prehistoric, then comes to Jesus, is radically transformed and has now become a real influence throughout the country of Suriname and into northern Brazil. And they want to use media to help do that. It's incredible what God has done through one family and how media through TWR is enhancing the platform to move throughout the Amazon region."

Steve Shantz, a longtime TWR missionary from Canada who is working closely with Tom on this project, echoes that sentiment. "It's probably not going to be the West that finishes the Great Commission but more likely the indigenous people groups who were once unreached taking the gospel to neighboring tribes and villages," he explained. "That's our dream in missions, and that's what the Wayana and Trio are doing."

"How blessed is the man who does not walk

in the counsel of the wicked, nor stand in the path of sinners,

nor sit in the seat of scoffers! But his delight is in the law

of the Lord, and in His law he meditates day and night.

He will be like a tree firmly planted by streams of water,

which yields its fruit in its season and its leaf does not wither;

and in whatever he does, he prospers."

— PSALM 1:1-3

26

From Denial to Doubt to Decision

R ACHID STARED AT the address he had scribbled on his hand. He was livid, having just heard on the radio what he considered blasphemies against Islam, all contradicting what he had been taught about the Christian faith and especially about Jesus Christ.

The program announcer had given an address for people to write to if they had questions or wanted to know more.

I'll show them that they're wrong, Rachid thought.

RACHID WAS BORN in 1971 and grew up in a small village in Morocco. His father was the imam of the local mosque. He was destined to follow in his dad's footsteps, being groomed to eventually take over. Beginning even at 4 years old, he focused on learning the fundamental tenets of Islam and memorizing the Quran.

"My dad was very strict about teaching the Quran," Rachid told Arabic Media Ministries. "He believed it was the word of Allah. Nobody should mess with it."

In a video interview with the organization Bridge to Muslims, he added, "My dad's joy was having a son who was going to lead and teach people about Islam and the Quran. That was my life, and I was happy with that."

Being the son of an imam brought Rachid a deep sense of pride – and status. He was convinced Islam was the true religion and the path to God.

Friction arose over where Rachid was to receive his education. It became a bone of contention between his father and mother. His dad wanted him to be educated strictly in the mosque. His mother pushed back, arguing that their son should attend "normal" school and receive a "secular" education. His mother prevailed on that front.

So, at the age of 12, Rachid moved to the bustling port city of Casablanca in western Morocco to live with his uncle. Economics and computer science piqued his interest.

A man carries a bundle as he walks down a path in Morocco. The Moroccan population is more than 99% Muslim, according to Joshua Project.

PHOTO BY AMY WENZEL

"I moved from a village of hundreds of people to a city of 3 million people," Rachid said. "It was like a different world."

But one thing didn't change. Rachid's uncle promised his father that the boy would continue attending the mosque and following the teachings of Islam.

"However, when I moved to Casablanca, I discovered different tools of entertainment and stuff like that," Rachid noted. "One of them was a radio."

Following dinner one evening after fasting during the day, Rachid picked it up and began tuning the dial to different stations. He was startled by an Arabic program talking about Jesus. Though promoting beliefs from the Bible, the program arrested Rachid's attention.

Rachid fumed, shaking his fist when he heard that Jesus was the Son of God and that he came to earth as a human being to die and save all humanity from their sins. He wanted to cover his ears. Yet, out of curiosity, he kept listening.

"I heard all the blasphemies for me as a Muslim," he shared in a TWR testimony video. "That [Jesus] was God himself appearing in the flesh. That he was crucified for our sins, taking them onto himself. This was insane. I was so full of anger because they were using the Arabic language. They spoke like us, but they were preaching a different message."

When the program ended, Rachid grabbed a pen and searched for a piece of paper to write down the address but couldn't find any. So he scrawled it on his hand, with the intention of writing and blasting away in an attempt to dissuade the on-air announcer from spouting blatantly false doctrine.

"The radio station I listened to was TWR," Rachid said.

THAT FIRST LETTER and subsequent reply a few weeks later began a four-year correspondence between Rachid and TWR. Unlike today, when people communicate instantly via social media, writing letters was the primary means of communication. A letter was the Facebook of that time, Rachid likes to say.

Over those 48 months, he compared and contrasted the teachings of Islam and Christianity. He peppered the TWR team with question after question. Repeatedly, he asked for a Bible, and the TWR team said they kept sending copies, though they mysteriously never arrived. But one day, the mailman delivered a Bible that had no cover, presumably concealing its identity from monitoring authorities.

Then he made a stunning conclusion. "I always tell people I don't know the exact timing of when I was born in faith," he said. "But I started doubting my Islamic faith and was leaning toward the Christian faith progressively." This was roughly 1990, when he turned 19.

He sent a letter to his friends at TWR and told them, "I think I'm a Christian, because I have nothing in Islam left."

Rachid had set out to disprove Christianity. But he ended up surrendering his life to Jesus Christ instead.

TWR connected him with an American missionary living in Morocco. They met in a downtown Casablanca coffeeshop. The missionary asked Rachid questions to draw out what he now believed.

"Who is God for you?" the man asked.

"God is the Creator," Rachid said.

"Who are we?"

"We are just human beings, his creation."

"Well, tell me then, who is Jesus?" the missionary continued.

"Jesus is God himself, incarnated in the flesh" was Rachid's answer.

"What did he do?"

"He was crucified for our sins."

"What is sin?"

"Sin is that thing that separates us from God."

"And you accept that?" the missionary posed.

"Yes. Jesus died for me," Rachid replied.

"Well, I think you're a Christian," the man said.

"Did they send you to test me or something?" Rachid protested, quite puzzled at this line of inquiry.

The missionary quickly reassured Rachid about his newfound commitment to Jesus. "No, no. I just wanted to make sure you understand the Christian faith. OK?" the missionary said. Rachid nodded.

The man invited Rachid to meet other Moroccan believers the next day. He was shocked. "I thought I was the only believer," he said. That

A boy kneels in front of the Hassan II Mosque in Casablanca. Rachid, who is not pictured, was sent to school in Casablanca when he was 12. "It was like a different world," he said.

PHOTO BY AMY WENZEL

afternoon Rachid couldn't believe his eyes. Here were other Moroccan men holding their Bibles and singing in the Moroccan language. "It was really something, like a dream," he told Bridge to Muslims.

Their story was the same. Radio via TWR. Correspondence courses. Coming to faith. "That's why I believe in the power of the gospel using media," Rachid said.

TROUBLE AROSE, THOUGH, when his uncle, his cousin and others noticed changes in Rachid's life. They wondered what was going on. Was he possibly turning his back on Islam?

One day, when Rachid arrived home, he was confronted heatedly by his family, including his mother. They asked him point blank: "Are you a Christian? Or are you a Muslim?" Rachid paused, thinking through his response. Finally, he said, "It's not your right to know what's in my heart, and you actually should not ask that question."

Weeping, his mother blurted, "Just tell them, just tell the Shahada [the Islamic creed], and make everybody know you are a Muslim, just say it in front of everybody!"

Ten seconds went by. Again Rachid measured what he would say. "Mom, I cannot say the Shahada." He would not deny Christ.

The room erupted. Some spat on him. Others cursed him. "You're a filthy dog." "You've brought shame on your father." "Get out of here. We don't want to see you." His mother wailed.

Rachid left, not knowing where to go. Tears trickled down his cheeks.

For the next two years, Rachid wandered, homeless. He drifted from place to place. "Sometimes I slept in the street because I didn't know where to go," he said. "I lost my studies. I lost my family. I lost everything."

But God did not abandon Rachid. A friend contacted him and notified him about a center in Cyprus, where he could rest and study the Bible. Rachid accepted the offer. "It was refreshing because I met other Muslim-background believers from Egypt, Jordan, Lebanon and other countries," he said. "I saw how God was working among other people like me."

RACHID WAS ABLE to wind his way back to Morocco. He started back to school at Hassan II University in Casablanca, and he worked at a company in accounting. He met his wife, also a Moroccan believer, in a summer Bible school, and they were married in 1997.

Then 26, he worked at rebuilding the damaged bridge to his family. He reached out to them, but his mother tried to rebuff his overture. "I told her that my God has taught me to love you more," Rachid said in his Arabic Media Ministries interview. He kept at it, showing and sharing with them the love of Christ.

An opportunity arose to minister with the Bible Society, smuggling Scriptures and Christian literature through Spain to Morocco. Rachid distributed them to Moroccans who were seeking to know more about Jesus. At the same time, he and his wife hosted meetings in their apartment with Muslim-background believers. "We stood for their rights and defended them, also helping them to find jobs," he said. "We ate a meal together. We didn't have much, but we were happy."

Danger followed him though. Someone posed as a Christian and infiltrated the home group. He sold the information to the secret police. Journalists also started writing scurrilous stories about him. The mosque next to their apartment preached against him on Fridays. "Every time I left our apartment, I'd look right and left before stepping outside, expecting somebody to come with a knife and stab me," he said.

Sensing God's prompting, Rachid and his wife fled Morocco for their safety. Again, God took care of them. This time, he received a phone call about wanting him to join a TV ministry. "I'm not a TV person," Rashid answered. His wife laughed. "Please pray and think about it for a month," the friend exhorted them.

So they did. God used Stephen's martyrdom recorded in the Book of Acts to speak to their hearts. The couple concluded: "If we Muslim-background believers don't preach the gospel to our people, who's going to do it? We will do it, no matter what it costs. We will appear on TV. We will share our faith even if it means giving our lives for that."

IN 2005, RACHID began hosting his own television show with Al Hayat TV. The goal was to encourage Muslims to ask questions, no matter how daring.

When the program debuted, he hoped 10 to 20 Muslims would call. They received 800 calls in the first half hour, shutting down the program's website because the server couldn't handle the load.

"When I read my first email and the person said, 'I had the same doubts and questions you had. After you gave your testimony, I accepted Christ,'" Rachid said. "I cried. There is a huge thirst. The harvest is there. We just need the workers."

That TV program ran until 2018. But Brother Rachid, as he's best known, continues to partner with other ministries to proclaim God's unending love across the Arab world – urging Muslims to place their hope in Jesus Christ.

TWR PRESIDENT LAUREN Libby remembers the first time he met Brother Rachid. He and the leader of ERF in Germany had driven to Virginia Beach to meet with leaders of the Christian Broadcasting Network. "The president of CBN, who was a good friend of mine and who used to listen to our programs while serving as a young soldier in Europe, said to me, 'I'd like to introduce to you one of your alumni. He came to Christ because of listening to TWR,'" Libby explained. "Out walked this striking Arab man. I praise the Lord, who took a series of TWR broadcasts and multiplied their impact many times over using Brother Rachid throughout the Muslim world. Only God can do that!"

Just as Rachid is doing – and as TWR is continuing to do – you can fulfill the gospel ministry to which God has called you. Prayerfully step out in faith. Stand for the truth. Reveal it. And trust the Lord to guide and provide. He will be faithful. He will use you to help advance his kingdom.

Let God write your story to his glory.

"My heart is steadfast, God, my heart is steadfast;

I will sing, yes, I will sing praises!

I will praise You, Lord, among the peoples;

I will sing praises to You among the nations.

For Your goodness is great to the heavens

and Your truth to the clouds.

Be exalted above the heavens, God;

may Your glory be above the earth."

– PSALM 57:7, 9-11

Epilogue

By Lauren Libby, TWR President

W HAT A PRIVILEGE it's been for me to serve as president and CEO of TWR since the Lord led me and my wife, June, to move in 2008 from Colorado Springs, Colorado, to Cary, North Carolina. We have been blessed so many times over as we've seen God at work around the world in the lives of so many people. I never tire of seeing him change lives. He is drawing men, women, boys and girls to himself – people who will spend eternity worshipping Jesus, their Lord who died for them on the cross so that they might have life forever more.

I stand in awe of God's wondrous, if not miraculous, provision, fulfilling his precious promises throughout Scripture. We have a policy that we strictly follow at TWR and that's not to go into debt for any project. We don't proceed until we have the funds on hand to cover it. God has always supplied the money – and the people and equipment – enabling us to accomplish what we sense God leading us to do. That's incredible when you think about it. But God owns everything and moves resources around as he sees fit. We're simply to trust him – as hard as that can be at times – and then to be wise stewards of the resources that he provides.

We want to be faithful to the mission to which God has clearly called us. One of my mentors used to lecture me to never forget the mission and always clearly articulate what that mission is. Well, for us at TWR, it's to

proclaim the good news of Jesus Christ to the whole world by mass media so that lasting fruit is produced.

Our purpose is not simply to build and manage an organization. We are to propagate the good news of Jesus Christ to the whole world. The wonderful thing about technology is that the world is becoming smaller and smaller. And so we have the opportunity to touch lives every day – from our neighbors' lives next door to others' lives in our city, our state, our country and ultimately throughout the world.

What we have tried to do through this book is to illustrate how God is big enough to take ordinary individuals from diverse backgrounds and to provide everything that is necessary to accomplish what he has called them to do.

This reminds me of how God used a similar book – about the founding of the Far East Broadcasting Company – in my life when I was in high school. I was a nonbeliever then, and yet I was fascinated with and captivated by all the miracles that God performed on behalf of the founders of FEBC. God, even back then, was beginning to move in my life in terms of what eventually he would have me and June do all these years later with our lives.

But you know, the Great Commission from our Lord Jesus Christ doesn't just apply to us here at TWR. Nor does it apply solely to North America, Europe, Asia, Africa or Latin America, or the Northern or Southern Hemispheres. Jesus commissioned every believer to go into all the world and proclaim the gospel to every person and to make disciples of all nations. He was speaking to people like you and me.

I get a bit emotional about it because it's an astounding privilege. It's the greatest movement in the history of the world. And we thank everyone who has served, partnered and supported the TWR ministry!

Just as we have at TWR, you, too, can step out in faith, looking to God for the mission he's calling you to and that he will provide all you need to fulfill that calling. You can be a part of his work.

Are you ready for him to work in your life and to use you in no small way? A God-sized adventure awaits you!

Appendix

Watt's Up?

A Primer on Radio Terminology

TWR is a multimedia ministry that began with radio and in which radio remains a significant aspect. The terminology used in radio may be unfamiliar and seem confusing to readers who don't live and breathe radio.

We turned to a couple of longtime TWR experts to help sort it out.

RADIO BANDS

In this book, we've primarily used the terms AM, FM and shortwave because these are the familiar terms to people in the United States. Bill Damick, retired after a long career with TWR, explained that much of the world uses the term medium wave instead of AM (which stands for amplitude modulation).

Whatever it's called, it generally operates between 525 and 1705 kilohertz.

AM radio's main strength is its reach, Damick said, although this varies depending on the level of power (see wattage discussion below) and other factors. Its weaknesses are that it is prone to electrical interference and doesn't give great fidelity for music.

FM (or frequency modulation) operates between 87.5 and 108 megahertz. FM's strengths are great fidelity for music broadcast and lower interference from electrical sources. It doesn't reach as far as AM or shortwave.

Shortwave operates between 2300 and 26100 kilohertz (or 2.3 and 26.1 megahertz). Its strength is its reach – it's reflected off the ionosphere, the layer of atmosphere that extends from 37 to 190 miles above the Earth's surface. As it "bounces" off the ionosphere, it can travel great distances.

The effectiveness of how well the ionosphere reflects radio signals is controlled by energy output from the sun and how it strikes the Earth. The sun's energy level rises and falls over 11-year cycles, and it also has sporadic energy bursts. These conditions, combined with the time of day, season and angle of the energy hitting the ionosphere, are broadly called "space weather."

Another weakness, Damick said, is that sales of shortwave radios have decreased markedly in most developed countries. However, the longer ranges achieved by shortwave or long-reaching AM are still the best way for TWR to reach some of its audiences. These can overcome geographic and political boundaries. It's not just TWR that still finds shortwave effective in some situations. Near the beginning of the war in Ukraine in 2022, the BBC started broadcasting into the war-torn country via shortwave, the *New York Times* reported. It was a way of ensuring that the flow of information would continue when Ukraine's communications infrastructure was under attack.

WATTAGES

In the TWR world, both "watts" and "kilowatts" are used. We've stuck with watts in this book. A kilowatt is simply a thousand watts. So, for example, a 500,000-watt transmitter would be a 500-kilowatt transmitter.

Dave Pedersen is a global broadcast engineer for TWR who previously served for nine years at our station on the island of Bonaire. "All things being equal, more power means more range," Pedersen said.

But a variety of factors play into how well a signal is received and heard by the listener. What counts is how well the desired signal is received, compared with how much unwanted interfering signals, or "noise," is working against reception quality.

The electronic noise level has increased enormously in the past 20 years, Pedersen said. Smart TVs, laptops, even LED light bulbs all produce "noise" that competes with radio waves. That's why Pedersen, who lives in South Texas, can use a good portable radio to pick up an AM signal from the TWR transmitter on Bonaire, 2,158 miles from his home – but only in his back lawn and not inside the house.

And only in the evening, because AM signals reach much farther at night than during the day. The reason goes back to the ionosphere, according to the Federal Communications Commission. AM signals can "bounce" off the ionosphere at night but not during the day. This is because of how the ionosphere itself behaves, not because of anything humans do. But it's why the FCC requires certain AM stations to go off the air at night or reduce power. It's trying to avoid a jumble of signals from two stations with the same frequency.

That's the same reason the maximum power allowed a U.S. AM radio station is 50,000 watts. Elsewhere, though, much higher power is allowed. You'll notice in this book that TWR uses transmitters with as much as a million watts of power.

What does that mean? Well, other things being equal, Pedersen offers these AM ranges according to wattage:

DAYTIME

- 10,000 watts – up to 250 miles
- 50,000 watts – up to 350 miles
- 500,000 watts – 400-500 miles
- (A million watts adds little more daytime reach.)

NIGHTTIME

- 10,000 watts – 500 miles
- 50,000 watts – 1,000 miles
- 500,000 watts – 2,500 miles
- 1 million watts – 3,500 miles

But many of TWR's transmitters can increase their reach because they are multidirectional as opposed to omnidirectional. The latter type sends its signals in all directions, whereas a multidirectional signal can be focused in a particular direction. "If you're in Bonaire, you don't want to broadcast into the ocean," Pedersen said. "If you want to reach up to Cuba, you'll point toward Cuba."

Picture it like lighting a room with a single standard light bulb in the middle of a room, he said. The whole room is lit, but the farthest parts are dimmer. If you are trying to read a book in a dim area, you could put in a more powerful light bulb, but that uses more expensive electricity. The other option is to use a spotlight of the same power focusing the light to where you are reading and not lighting parts of the room that do not have anyone else in them.

A final factor, Pedersen said, is the quality of the radio. Although some high-quality AM radios are made today, most are not good quality but are more affordable. So if TWR is distributing radios in an area where our signal is strong, we'll opt for lower-quality radios because we can purchase more for the same amount of money. But if the signal is weaker, we have to provide higher-quality radios, or the message won't be heard at all.

DRM, which stands for Digital Radio Mondiale and is often referred to as digital broadcasting, enables the delivery of audio programming, PDF transmission or sending the Bible and materials over thousands of miles via digital radio transmissions.

Bibliography

CHAPTER 1: "Rescued From a Notorious Drug Kingpin"

- In-depth interview with Carlos Yepes by TWR's video team

CHAPTER 2: "Lasting Fruit, Beginning in Spain"

- Freed, Dr. Paul E. *Towers to Eternity.* Nashville, Tennessee: Thomas Nelson Inc. Publishers, 1994. First published 1967.

- Personal newsletters from Dr. Freed to supporters and friends

- Youth for Christ International: "Celebrating 77 Years and Beyond – Since 1944"

- "The Surprising Work of God" by Garth Rosell

CHAPTER 3: "A Secret Listener Takes the Risk"

- Email interview with Berti Dosti

- Butterworth, John. *God's Secret Listener.* La Grange, Kentucky: 10Publishing, 2022.

CHAPTER 4: "Caribbean Miracles"

- In-person interviews with Joe Barker; Tim Klingbeil, both in Cary, N.C.

- Reflections taken from *Footsteps* interview with Lauren Libby by Andy Napier

CHAPTER 5: "Tiny Nation, Big Pulpit"

- *Great Things He Has Done: A Testimony of God's Faithfulness Through 60 Years of TWR Media Ministry.* Cary, N.C.: Trans World Radio, 2014.

- Video interviews with Bill Mial; Sphiwe Nxumalo-Ngwenya and Steve Stavropoulos; Juliet Oppong-Amoako

- Swaziland transmitter 20th anniversary booklet

- "Swaziland Transmitter Dedication," 2016 video by Andrew Haas

- Reflections taken from *Footsteps* interview with Lauren Libby by Andy Napier

- "The Real Story Behind Britain's Rock 'n' Roll Pirates," National Public Radio, Nov. 13, 2009; "Part 1: The Pirates," from "Radio Reinvented" in "History of the BBC"

CHAPTER 6: "Through Storms, Building a Secure Future on Guam"

- In-person interviews with Joe Barker; Tim Klingbeil, both in Cary, N.C.

- Video interview with Daryl Renshaw

- Email interview with Darin Alvord

- Updates from KTWR on Guam

- News articles from TWR.org

- TWR listener reports

CHAPTER 7: "Seed Planters in Japan's Hard Soil"

- Video interview with Samuel Tan

- Video conference with Aaron Tan, Jonathan Lee and Leanne Tan

- Video conference with Hirotaka Sasaki, Jonathan Chen, Pastor Park Sang Bum and Junki Sugiyama

- Reflections taken from *Footsteps* interview with Lauren Libby by Andy Napier

- Joshua Project website

- National Geographic online: "Mar 11, 2011 CE: Tohoku Earthquake and Tsunami"

- Mike and Dana Ball, prayer letter to supporters, July 2022, and additional reflections from Mike Ball

- In-person interview with Werner Kroemer, Bratislava, Slovakia

- In-person interview with Lauren Libby, Cary, N.C.

- TWR listener reports

CHAPTER 8: "Hope in a Cuban Sugar-Cane Field"

- González Muñoz, Alberto I. *God Doesn't Come in My Office: Struggling With Bitterness When We Are Victims of Injustice.* Frisco, Texas: ABG Ministries, 2012.

- Interview of Alberto with Andy Napier, host of TWR's *Footsteps*

- Interview of Alberto with Byron Tyler, host of Bott Radio Network's *Mid-South Viewpoint*

CHAPTER 9: "A Voice for the Gospel in Times of War"

- Video interview with Nick Siemens

- In-person interview with Maria Wedel, Bratislava, Slovakia

- Reports from TWR Ukraine

- Reporting on the Ukraine-Russia crisis by TWR Marketing and Communications teams in Europe and the U.S.

CHAPTER 10: "A Special Heart and Burden for Nigeria"

- Video interviews with Garth Kennedy; Branko Bjelajac

- Email interview with Abdoulaye Sangho

- Open Doors' 2022/2023/2024 World Watch List

- Decision Magazine online: "Nov. 8, 2023 Nigeria Named Most Dangerous Nation for Christians"

- Rittenhouse, Flora. *Reaching Beyond Barriers: A Legacy of Hope.* Kempton Park, South Africa: Trans World Radio Africa, 2009.

- TWR listener reports

- Reflections taken from *Footsteps* interview with Lauren Libby by Andy Napier

CHAPTER 11: "The Secret Towers"

- Mike and Dana Ball, prayer letter to supporters, July 2022, and additional reflections from Mike Ball.

- In-person interview with Werner Kroemer, Bratislava, Slovakia

- In-person interview with Lauren Libby, Cary, N.C.

- TWR listener reports

CHAPTER 12: "God's Love and Care Are Evident in Central Asia"

- TWR listener reports

CHAPTER 13: "Economic Calamity Can't Halt Ministry"

- TWR.org news article: "TWR Lanka Strengthens Churches with Radio Homes"

- TWR.org news article: "Despite Difficulties, TWR Team Faithfully Ministering in Sri Lanka"

- CNN: "Sri Lanka Is Facing an Economic and Political Crisis" (April 6, 2022)

- PBS News Hour: "Sri Lankans Demand Justice Three Years After Easter Massacre" (April 17, 2022)

- Gisreportsonline.com: "Sri Lanka Struggles to Recover Economically" (Oct. 18, 2022)

- New York Times: "For Sri Lanka, a Long History of Violence" (April 21, 2019)

- TWR listener reports

CHAPTER 14: "Reaching Behind Closed Doors"

- TWR listener reports

CHAPTER 15: "Bringing Light to Women"

- Video interview with Peggy Banks

- Spieker, Marli. *When Hope Wins.* Cary, N.C.: Trans World Radio, 2010.

- TWR listener reports, including Kabyle Women of Hope story

- TWR.org news article: "Bringing Hope to Women in a Broken World"

CHAPTER 16: "Compassion Extended to the Roma People"

- In-person interviews with Werner Kroemer; Samuel Lacho, both in Bratislava, Slovakia

- TWR listener reports

- Council of Europe online: "Roma and Travellers"

- Amnesty International media briefing, "Europe: Discrimination Against Roma," Oct. 27, 2007

- New World Encyclopedia: Roma

CHAPTER 17: "Men of Valor and Courage"

- In-person interviews with Caleb Petersen*; Lonnie Berger; Sterling Ottun, all in Cary, N.C.

CHAPTER 18: "A Unique Opportunity for Southeast Asia"

- Video interview with Daryl Renshaw

- Interview with Eugene Lim

- TWR.org news article: "TWR Affiliates with SE Asian Station to Expand Gospel Outreach"

- TWR listener reports

CHAPTER 19: "Expanding Commitment to the Horn of Africa"

- TWR Magazine news article "The Horn of Africa Needs Jesus"

- TWR listener reports

CHAPTER 20: "Turning Toward Humanitarian Crises"

- Video interviews with Bernice Gatere; Bill Mial

- In-person interview with Tom Watkins, Cary, N.C.

- Reflections taken from *Footsteps* interview with Lauren Libby by Andy Napier

- Michael Buerk report from Ethiopia on BBC News, Oct. 23, 1984

- UNAIDS fact sheet 2022, "Global AIDS Statistics"

- U.S. Centers for Disease Control and Prevention fact sheet, "HIV remains a leading cause of death worldwide," February 2022

- World Health Organization, African Region: HIV/Aids, 2021

- Ministry of Health, Republic of Uganda, "Uganda reports significant drop in mother to child HIV infections," May 31, 2022

CHAPTER 21: "The Gift of Genuine Friendship"

- Email interview with Scott A. Jones

- Telephone interviews with John Summerville; Paul Harkness; Andy Napier; Larry and Patti Souder; James Baker; John Owens

CHAPTER 22: "Living Water to New Generations"

- In-person interview with Ralf Stores; Tom Streeter, both in Cary, N.C.

CHAPTER 23: "Sharing the Story via Video"

- Video interviews with Aicha*; Tyler Gates

- In-person interview with Candace Mackie, Cary, N.C.

A pseudonym for security reasons

CHAPTER 24: "Telling the Story in a Fresh Way"

- In-person interviews with Luiz Sayão; Esteban Larrosa, both in Cary, N.C.

- Transcript of signing ceremony at TWR U.S. headquarters, March 22, 2023

- TWR global reports from Africa and Asia

CHAPTER 25: "The Unreached Are Not Forgotten"

- In-person interview with Jon Fugler, Cary, N.C.

- TWR.org news articles: "TWR Builds This Gospel Partnership on a ROCK" and "How TWR Invests in Unreached People"

- *TWR Magazine* news article, "Helping Amazon Tribes Minister Via Radio"

- TWR listener reports

CHAPTER 26: "From Denial to Doubt to Decision"

- Rachid video interviews with Arabic Media Ministries; TWR; Bridge to Muslims

APPENDIX: "Watt's Up"

- Video interviews with Bill Damick; Dave Pedersen

About the Authors

Richard Greene, originally from Wilmington, Delaware, is a longtime journalist. He committed his life to Christ at the University of Tennessee, Knoxville. He first worked as a reporter and church editor with the Chattanooga News-Free Press, then served as a writer and editor with The Navigators, the Billy Graham Evangelistic Association, TWR, Smith & Associates and Samaritan's Purse. He's traveled to 64 countries. With Jim and Linda Jones of Sylacauga, Alabama, he co-authored "If You Distribute, I Will Provide: One Couple's Call to Trust God to Feed Hungry Children." He and his wife, Lynda, live in Boone, North Carolina. They have two grown daughters, three granddaughters and one grandson.

A native of Estherville, Iowa, **John Lundy** came to faith in Christ as a young boy and experienced a deepening personal relationship with Jesus through fellow students at the University of Missouri-Columbia and through a church in Michigan City, Indiana. He has a bachelor's degree in journalism from Missouri and had a 40-year newspaper career in Indiana, Ohio and Duluth, Minnesota. Sensing a call to a late-career missions assignment, he connected with TWR. After 13 months of raising a ministry partnership team, he came to TWR in January 2022 as a writer and editor in the Cary, North Carolina, office. He's single and lives in Cary, North Carolina.

Making Waves With Technology...

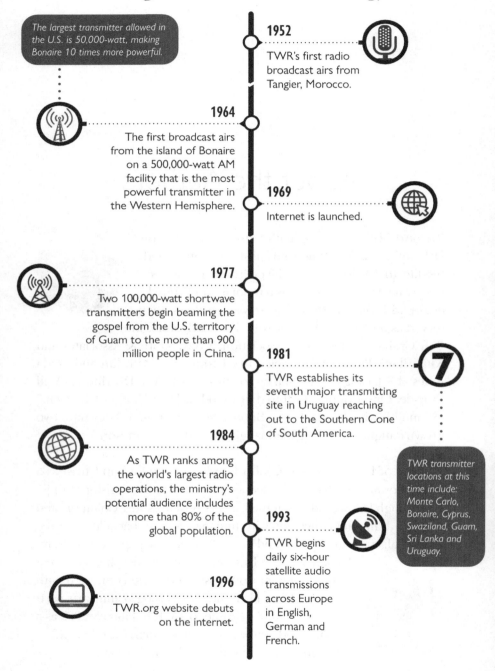

The largest transmitter allowed in the U.S. is 50,000-watt, making Bonaire 10 times more powerful.

1952
TWR's first radio broadcast airs from Tangier, Morocco.

1964
The first broadcast airs from the island of Bonaire on a 500,000-watt AM facility that is the most powerful transmitter in the Western Hemisphere.

1969
Internet is launched.

1977
Two 100,000-watt shortwave transmitters begin beaming the gospel from the U.S. territory of Guam to the more than 900 million people in China.

1981
TWR establishes its seventh major transmitting site in Uruguay reaching out to the Southern Cone of South America.

1984
As TWR ranks among the world's largest radio operations, the ministry's potential audience includes more than 80% of the global population.

TWR transmitter locations at this time include: Monte Carlo, Bonaire, Cyprus, Swaziland, Guam, Sri Lanka and Uruguay.

1993
TWR begins daily six-hour satellite audio transmissions across Europe in English, German and French.

1996
TWR.org website debuts on the internet.

...to Speak Hope to the World

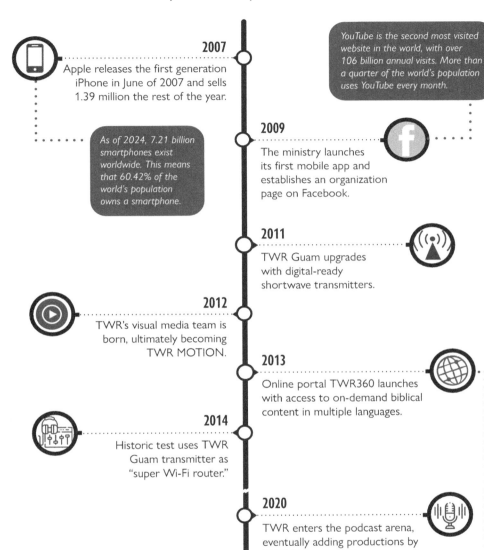

2007

Apple releases the first generation iPhone in June of 2007 and sells 1.39 million the rest of the year.

YouTube is the second most visited website in the world, with over 106 billion annual visits. More than a quarter of the world's population uses YouTube every month.

As of 2024, 7.21 billion smartphones exist worldwide. This means that 60.42% of the world's population owns a smartphone.

2009

The ministry launches its first mobile app and establishes an organization page on Facebook.

2011

TWR Guam upgrades with digital-ready shortwave transmitters.

2012

TWR's visual media team is born, ultimately becoming TWR MOTION.

2013

Online portal TWR360 launches with access to on-demand biblical content in multiple languages.

2014

Historic test uses TWR Guam transmitter as "super Wi-Fi router."

2020

TWR enters the podcast arena, eventually adding productions by TWR Women of Hope; national partners in Spain, Latin America and Ukraine; TWR MOTION; and others.

2024

TWR receives the esteemed Billy Graham Award for Excellence in Christian Communications at the National Religious Broadcasters convention in Nashville, Tennessee.

TWR360 began with content in five languages and has grown to include more than 140 languages today.

Made in the USA
Middletown, DE
02 September 2024

60252283R00146